Josephine's Jamaican Journey

Short Stories
Book 1 - In Di Yaad

Joan P. Hamilton

Josephine's Jamaican Journey - Book One - In Di Yaad

Published in the UK by SelectArrow Ltd. www.selectarrow.net
Email: office.selectarrow@gmail.com

ISBN: 978-1-7398830-3-4

Cover and interior design: Homer Slack
Editor: Angela B. Slack

Dedication

This collection of short stories is dedicated to my mother and father (each now deceased) and my two beautiful grandchildren, Ava and Noah.

"Tin-Tin" or Kelsada Maragh (without fanfare) lived her life for her children. She showed us what love, kindness to others, hard work, contentment and integrity looked like, amid relative hardships.

"Alty" or Altamont St James McDonald was a loving father whose presence in our lives helped to anchor us emotionally rather than make us adrift in a sea of emotional *'what ifs.'* We knew him, loved him, and knew that he loved us despite his deficits. To my mind, my father triumphed in later life, becoming a distinguished older man whose grandchildren adored him. He never stopped learning to be a better man.

My darling grandchildren, Ava and Noah, may you recognise your rich legacy in these writings. As you grow up in a different time and culture, you may realise early that differences in financial and cultural circumstances should not become barriers to being the best version of yourselves. You have in your DNA the grit and drive to overcome any odds that life throws in front of you. May you be proud of who you are and from whom you are descended.

Lastly, may you know, above all else, that God is your source of life, no matter the circumstance.

Acknowledgement

This work is 63 years in the making, the last 23 of which had me penning the stories. Over time, many people encouraged me to present the stories in book form. On a lark, I shared a few stories with my dear friend and mentor of nearly 40 years, Velmore Lawrence, who 'set the ball in motion.' Thank you for sharing my stories with Homer and Angela Slack, my publishers and introducing me to them. You have been a 'cheerleader' in my life.

To Angela, my patient and hardworking editor, this has been a fun ride! I have finally found what I enjoy doing. Your guidance and knowledge have been inspiring, and I am so grateful that the Lord brought you and Homer into my life. Thank you.

To Homer, your technical support and management of the designs and illustrations used in the stories have me marvelling at what can be achieved by the collaborative effort of individuals with varying talents and gifts to benefit a joint undertaking.

I was moved to tears when you presented Josephine's likeness to me. Despite the stories, I had no image in mind of how she might be portrayed, and as soon as I saw what you presented, It resonated with me at a deeper level. Thank you both.

To my family, Arthur, Rory, Lee and Rachel, my heartfelt thanks for making my life so rich. I have enjoyed being a pampered' wife by Arthur, who after many years remains 'my best gift from God' and 'my strong man'.

To my children, it's been a joy to be a parent to each of you in different ways and for different reasons. Each of you has inspired me to reach deeper into myself to understand and relate to others. You've each 'forced' me to pray, trust God, and believe with greater faith His promises, as my love for each of you compels me to seek help for what matters to me. I love each of you so very much.

My sister Janice, I am often reminded that you are the person I have known and loved the longest. Thank you for being the feet I watched under the blackboard on my first school day. I was not alone as long as I could see your feet. That feeling has obtained throughout my life. You uniquely know and share with me as family.

As I was known in primary school, I remain Janice McDonald's sister and president of your fan club. I thought I could not love you more than when we were growing up together; I was wrong. Each day brings more respect, appreciation and love for you.

Lastly, my most recent discoveries of what love means are Ava and Noah, my grandchildren. Grandma hopes these stories will serve you well when she is no longer physically present. May you find 'nuggets of wisdom', slivers of insight and continuity of your lineage each time you refer to the stories that I will have shared.

Commit to the Lord whatever you do; He will establish your plans. Proverbs 16:3 NIV.

God is Love, and whoever abides in love abides in God, and God abides in him. 1 John 4:16 NIV

Endorsement

Joan Hamilton takes the reader into the mind of a little girl, Josephine, who is spirited, curious, active, imaginative and full of adventure. The reader 'travels' back to a time in Jamaica when life seemed simpler.

This story will resonate well with anyone who grew up in Jamaica in the fifties/sixties. It will deliver memories of fun times and hard times and yet a time in Jamaica when the village was there to care for those in the community, and people were more caring and gentler in spirit and deed.

Those of you in the diaspora will also be delighted to have this collection of short stories to enrich yourselves culturally and to help preserve our history by sharing it with the present generation.

Joan P. Hamilton's description of how people interacted in such proximity highlights many colourful and humorous examples as she makes the 'Tenement Yaad' come alive. Her astute description of the diversity of the characters in the 'Yaad' allows the reader to glimpse the often complex personalities of the characters. The author's recollections of events and happenings 'behind the scenes' in the community showcase the effect of communal life on behaviour in the broader social context and provide a rich and in-depth depiction of Jamaica in the 1960s.

As Josephine describes the various characters, one cannot help but observe that she may have been left alone quite often, being the youngest child in her family, and based on her description of her relationship with the mango tree, she may have been a lonely little girl.

Nevertheless, her quest to know and understand her world provided her with meaningful insights into the hearts of the people around her. Josephine had a natural love and curiosity for the people she interfaced with. So, despite her feelings of being bullied by her older sibling, Carla and her friend, she still maintained a fondness for each of them.

As the older sibling, this book has reminded me of a simpler time of life for us as children and the wealth people can still possess despite a lack of material things. Those days of running around without a care in the world, playing tricks on each other, were and are priceless.

I am, among many others, happy that Joan has finally decided to publish these stories that she has been writing for many years. Sharing these treasured memories with others in written form is sharing the blessing of real people and real memories of a bygone time in Jamaica that are invaluable. You are in for a real treat; join Josephine and her dynamic list of characters on her Jamaican journey.

Mrs Janice A. Lee [Sister],
Author/Entrepreneur,
St. Andrew,
Jamaica, West Indies.

Endorsement

Josephines' Jamaican Journey, Book 1 - In Di Yaad, is delightfully vivid, emotive and entertaining. This collection of short stories depicting life in Jamaica is coloured by authentic characters and experiences, as seen from the perspective of little Josephine. The storytelling pulls you in and makes this book relatable to everyone's childhood. The setting of our lives may differ, but the themes of sibling rivalry, growing up, and adult interpersonal relationships are all the same.

The 'Tenement Yard' anecdote transported me back to when I would visit my sister *"Tin-Tin"* and her family. This account is vibrantly descriptive of living conditions in a 1960s Kingston tenement with insightful deductions from Josephine. From the chickens in the yard to the gossips under the mango tree, the narrative takes us on a journey that could take place anywhere in the world but adds Jamaican flavour.

If you are interested in delving into Jamaican culture and understanding how the nation grew from independence to nationhood, Josephine gives insightful details of how she saw it unfold. You will love 'her take' on events and the characters as much as I did.

Grace Byrd
Retired Bilingual Chairperson,
Teacher of English as a Second Language,
Miami Dade County, Public Schools,
Florida, USA.

Endorsement

*Joan P. Hamilton's Josephine's Jamaican Journey - **Book One*** makes those who can identify with unstructured childhood feel a sense of accomplishment and completeness. Little Josephine's vivid recapturing of her childhood fantasies provides creative, fascinating, and engaging reading.

This attractively presented, reflective engagement in Josephine's childhood reality exposes those for whom modernity, sophistication and exposure to carefully orchestrated family socialisation is the norm, an opportunity to appreciate the value and virtues of a humble beginning and proper parenting.

A child's life through the eyes of Josephine's stories unfolded among intercultural siblings, creating an almost redefining appreciation of true childhood happiness. It underscores the traditional philosophical paradigm that true happiness does not lie in wealth or privilege.

The distinctive 'Tenement Yaad' setting of Josephine's development, reflected in the characteristic conflicting values, diverse behaviours and influences, provides exciting suspense. The compelling diversity of moods experienced in this collection's short narrative makes its reading a gripping and memorable experience.

The PHCC
Transforming Lives
Through The Power and Ministry of Jesus Christ
Bishop Dr. Alvin R. Bailey

Endorsement

The life of Christ and most Biblical characters are recorded in the narrative genre, each story unfolding a picturesque view of their lives, painting vividly the activities they participated in and persons encountered and the resultant effect on them. Like viewing recordings of their historical existence, their stories conjure a phantasmagoria of challenge and intrigue that replay for the readers, transporting them to the past.

Josephine's Jamaican Journey - Book One chronicles the memoirs of the childhood life and times of author Joan P. Hamilton, seen through the innocent eyes of a child. It is compiled as a collection of personal short stories that convey many emotions that will engage its readers to reminisce, each infused with humour and filled with golden nuggets confronting us to embrace the past as it is the foundation of our life in the present.

Despite circumstances of impoverishment and parents of different ethnicities, Josephine basked in the security of a loving family and caring sister. She articulately recounts the challenges brought about by her extended relatives and the difficulties encountered in navigating in-law relationships. Her stints of handling her father's inebriety are sobering, a twelve-year-old child in an adult's role. Many will align with her efforts and sympathise with her experiences.

'The Tenement Yard' is her memoir of her interactions with the people who resided with her in different sections there. The author's honesty and seeming simplicity are revealed in her incorporation of characters such as Uncle Keith, who was determined to enforce the racial disparity between the children, establishing who was a 'niega' and who was a 'Coolie.'

There was 'Miss Beryl the Beater,' an enforcer whose obsession for discipline influenced all who dwelled in 'The Tenement Yard.' The tenement yard manifested the African proverb, 'It takes a village', as all the adults shared in raising the children with the accompanying respect given to legal guardians and parents.

Then there were the hilarious antics surrounding Ms. Sheila, the visiting sales lady with the twisted wig who didn't have a man and her formidable impressions on young Josephine.

Josephine's childhood innocence is amplified by her conversations with her imaginary best friend, the mango tree and her deep care for the shaggy, mongrel puppy that was crippled as she sought divine intervention for its healing and care. Answered prayers for healing led to a deepening and sustaining of her faith into maturity, a prime example of how childhood experiences develop the convictions and regime of adults.

The individual stories contain such vivid material that we are presented with a kaleidoscope of family life. The book is a 'must read', and though entrancing, it is about the values created in local communities through the principles and lifestyles of those surrounding us and the lasting difference made in forging our lives.

Pastor Barrington Hall,
Ekklesia Bible Fellowship,
Kingston, Jamaica

Foreword

My purpose in writing this foreword is to engage you, the reader and encourage you to read this book. I pondered how to write to prove that this collection of short portrayals of life in a series is worth reading. Considering the objective a little differently, what will you appreciate from this book, and why am I appropriate to present any insights towards such an appreciation?

It is easier to answer the second question first. I happen to be the husband (for 41+ years) of the author, the real-life, 'Josephine', whose character (as a young person) is brought to life by her endearing recollections. Considering my sojourn with Joan during her adulthood, learning about her childhood years and experiences, her make-up as a woman and her general persona, I am more than qualified to invite you, the reader, into Josephine's world.

To meet the challenge of answering the first question, you will observe that the accounts of Joan P. Hamilton, chronicled in *Josephine's Jamaican Journey- Book One,* describe her experiences growing up in an underprivileged community within Kingston, Jamaica. She reveals the socioeconomic and political facts concerning the lives of persons in communities of this nature in immediate post-independence Jamaica. Joan P. Hamilton presents the reader with segments of her life as an individual whose life trajectory allowed her to graduate from struggling social circumstances in an under-served community to enjoy an adult life among the more comfortably 'well-off' in Jamaica. Her success story realises the promise of that which is achievable when a life is lived based on faith in God. Joan P. Hamilton inadvertently presents us with the evidence that God delivers on His covenant to be *Jehovah Jireh* to those who believe.

Perhaps with no surprise to those who know the author, she has stayed true to the persona that she possessed as a young child by maintaining and nurturing the characteristics that define her as a person, visibly and palpably caring, to a fault, about the welfare of others, being satisfied with less physical possessions and trappings than others would wish for, always embracing that kindness to fellow human beings and animals are more important than the markers used by western societies to describe achievement and status. All these characteristics and traits are underpinned by her deep faith in her God and His Son, Jesus Christ.

Joan transports readers to *The Tenement Yaad* in the then-underprivileged community in Kingston, Jamaica, which was home to Josephine for many years. The facilities (some communal) and the day-to-day way of living without 'uptown' comforts that outline the existence of those in these communities, then and now, are on full display. Yet to many, including Josephine, this was life; this is what she knew and could enjoy within the social grouping in such communities in Jamaica.

Josephine was not an unhappy child, not at all. She had family, and her community loved her. She found delight in various things that were features of her community life, the animals, the various characters who (because of their personality or behaviour) assumed a particular prominence in *The Tenement Yaad,* and in listening to the accounts of persons as they related their experiences in the areas outside of her immediate community and more.

In an age where historical experiences of bygone generations may be losing importance, chronologies of earlier times, no matter how presented, help to keep the threads of connection through the generations intact for the history of it all. In the case of Josephine's recollections, the lighter side of *The Tenement Yaad* living in Jamaica is richly preserved. The portrayals by the author in her series of recollections are full of life, and the narrative is wonderfully depictive, supported by illustrations that help to situate the reader in each place Josephine chooses to present to the reader.

The series will aid in a deeper appreciation of Caribbean culture for both young and old. The playful reminiscing by the author will indulge many in the diaspora (from all walks of life) as if Jamaican pantomime had come alive again but in book form.

Enjoy the company of Josephine and the cast of characters in *The Tenement Yaad* as she remembers.

I wholeheartedly recommend it.

Arthur Hamilton,
Attorney at Law,
St Andrew, Jamaica,
West Indies.

Contents

Stories   **Page**

Introduction

The stories that are contained in this volume are autobiographical. They are pure in interpreting situations as they happened around Josephine as a child. The stories cover a period of Josephine's life from age 4 through to 12 years old. Over this period, Josephine lived in four locations, all close to Spanish Town Road and Payne Avenue, in Kingston, Jamaica.

Josephine was always small for her age, a fact she worried about. Her feet were not big enough, and she was too skinny. Confoundingly, people would assume her to be younger than she was. To confirm her fears, her parents and the neighbours would administer and suggest various vitamins and potions to help her '*grow.*'

Despite what everyone thought or had to say, Josephine was just fine; she grew into a regular-sized person. She had a little nose with a natural pointy tip. A squarish face was embellished with a few freckles pointed out to her by an inquisitive boy at school. Josephine had brown eyes through which she saw 'everything.'

As she grew older, the freckles disappeared; she need not have worried about those either. Josephine's impression of how she appeared was mainly due to how others saw her. For example, Josephine understood from a toddler's observation that her complexion was like the colour of caramel.

Josephine had curly hair that seemed to defy all attempts to tame it. Ribbons or barrettes would slide off the hair. 'Unruly and untidy' were the words used to describe Josephine's hair until she found that an elastic band wound around her ponytail did the trick. However, getting the elastic band off the hair usually required Josephine's sister's help to cut it out.

Josephine loved being herself; she was fearless, brave, and very observant. She learned early to look out for herself and her sister. Josephine was bright, kind, confident and strong. Operating in a world where children were *to be seen and not heard'*, she found that she had a voice, and even when she did not speak, she could not mask her opinion. She recalls standing up for herself and her sister numerous times, even to adults.

Josephine was a happy child; she knew that her parents and God loved her. Her mother pronounced many good words over her, and her father was a loving dad when he was present. Papa had personal issues that caused him to drink to excess and be absent on occasions.

According to Josephine's mother, the doctors had told her that the pregnancy with Josephine was too precarious and would not end positively. Her mother referred to her often as a miracle. Josephine figured that God must have loved her as He allowed her to be born and then answered her prayers. Josephine was told all this by her mother, who said that she was such a fine girl that she could even visit and spend the night at the queen's palace because her manners were so good.

Josephine found that people were fascinating. She loved writing compositions at school and enjoyed getting lost in reading. She attended Cockburn Pen All-Age School at 3 Miles, Spanish Town Road, where it intersected with Hagley Park Road. Every Thursday, Josephine walked to the old Court House in Half Way Tree to collect three books from the library, and through books, she further nurtured her growing vocabulary, powers of expression, and fertile imagination.

Note to Parents and Teachers

Truly, Josephine is thankful for the teachers she had contact with; all except one proved to be affirming. The one exception happened in high school for the subject Spanish. The teacher said, "You will never amount to much." What a negative declaration to make about a child? Thanks be to God that Josephine did not wear that 'garment.' Instead, she remembers one teacher, Mrs Eloida V. Grant, saying to an education inspector one day while looking straight at Josephine, "It's not where they are coming from; it's where they are going."

Ironically, the Spanish that Josephine remembers in adult life is what she did not understand at the time of the negative pronouncement. Each unique person presents with differences in learning style, timing and readiness. This understanding must be foremost when adults deal with children when we guide them rather than expect them to follow a script or curriculum strictly. What beautiful opportunities adults, parents, teachers and mentors have to speak life-affirming messages to children.

Telling Josephine's stories of growing up in Jamaica during the 1960s allows us to see the importance of giving children the tool of self-expression. Children constantly observe and interpret their environment; let us remember that as we guide them. Josephine's 'Angel' Uncle John often reminded his sister Loris, *'No beat 'im tiday,'* that is to say, do not spank the baby today. Instead, let us be gentle with children. They are little people with all the emotions and feelings of adults. Let us invest in their imaginations by engaging their childlikeness and crouching down literally and figuratively to engage them face-to-face as we learn from them. I believe our inner child will be reawakened in the process.

Josephine liked people-watching. Good storytelling is still an attribute that she enjoys in those who can relate a story well. She enjoyed growing up in Jamaica. She still finds Patios and Jamaican cultural nuances to be novel. Jamaica is a 'real place', and Josephine is proud to be Jamaican. So, as you explore Jamaica through her inquisitive, childlike eyes, think critically and empathetically as you watch Josephine grow up along with the newly independent Jamaica.

MEET THE FAMILY

Josephine's family was initially just Mama, affectionately called *Tin-Tin*, Papa, otherwise called *Alty* and Carla, her older sister, two pillars and a stone; she called her family. The family lived in a room on McKoy Lane that ran off Spanish Town Road between the Two Miles and Three Miles markers. It was a dirt lane that did not see much vehicular traffic. Instead, people, donkey carts, and herds of cows used the lane daily to access their dwellings. The entire lane length was bordered on both sides by zinc fences in varying shades of rust. The fences had gates in them that led to yards. Wooden structures that served as homes. Some were nicer than others, with verandahs, fretwork and wooden louvred windows.

Josephine's memories of living in the lane are of the cows crowding out anyone when they were being moved. The mess they made, the smell of cow dung, the buzz of insects that are ever present when cows are about, and not wanting to get too close to them. Life on the lane was also communal as there was a *standpipe* where people went to fetch water. The family did not stay in that location for long as they moved while Josephine was still very young to Spanish Town Road, to a big yard, where Mama worked in a shop and bar, and the family lived in the back.

Born in 1929, Papa was tall and good-looking with light brown eyes. He walked with a gait, suggesting he was on top of the world. He was christened Altamont St James McDonald. When Mama was brave enough, she would imply sarcastically that he was not a saint even though he served as an Acolyte in the Anglican Church when he was younger.

Mama was short, with long hair and a face that was a bit angular but not square or round; she was pretty. Born in 1926, her family told her, her name was Kelsada Delores Maragh. This name was the one she lived and died with. However, Josephine and Carla had done extensive searches for a birth certificate for her to allow her to travel abroad, and they were never able to find the record of her birth. Years after she passed away, the family discovered that she was registered as Roslyn Rondas by the overseer of the estate that her mother lived on. The Indians did not read or write, and so the responsibility to register births fell to the overseer. Mama's father's name was Ramdas Maragh, and for whatever reason, the child was named Roslyn Rondas. Josephine thinks *Tin-Tin* would have found it hilarious had she known.

Josephine's first real memory of her family was of being carried in Papa's arms while Mama held Carla by the hand at what must have been a social event. Being high up in Papa's arms allowed her to see the people milling around as they listened to music blaring from speaker boxes and ate what might have been roasted corn and other treats found at such affairs. The outing was at twilight, so street lights were turned on, and the smoke from the cooking fires created clouds as the light and the smoke mingled in the air. Papa was young and strong then, so Josephine's perch felt sturdy. She also strongly sensed that Mama's hold on Carla was deliberate. There was no way she was going to let her wander off. The memory is fleeting in imagery, but it has set a tone of togetherness, safety, and love regarding her family in Josephine's heart.

Other fleeting memories confirmed for Josephine that her family loved and cared for her; Papa carried her on his shoulders as he walked through McKoy Lane, enquiring because someone on a bicycle 'hit down' Josephine earlier in the day. Riding high on his shoulder gave her a deep sense of security. *"You know a who nearly hurt mi pickney tiday?"* He asked a vendor by the entrance to the lane. Not getting a satisfactory answer, he persisted up the lane, asking other people. As Papa made his enquiries, his voice was angry and resolute about how he would deal with the offender. Thankfully, the culprit was never identified.

Another memory was Mama taking her to school and reminding her that she would collect her later that afternoon. In soft, reassuring tones, Mama spoke to Josephine. *"Mi ago come back fi yu later, no cry."*

On another occasion, Mama mistakenly took the number 7 - JOS bus going in the opposite direction to Spanish Town Road. Instead, they rode the bus to Papine and then back to Three Miles after a party at her boss's house in Havendale. *"Why it a tek* so long to get to Three Miles?" Mama asked the conductor. "You took the bus on the wrong side of the street," he told her. "Remain on the bus, and it will turn around and return to Three Miles," he said. Mama must have been such a picture; she was on a joy ride with two tired, sleepy little girls.

She was a loving, caring mother. Being only 4 feet 11 inches tall, *Tin-Tin* struggled to carry a growing child, but Josephine remembers that her mother carried her many times, once to the *Bustamante Children's Hospital*, where they spent most of the day. Having to retake the bus home, she had a sleeping Josephine in her arms.

Tired and worn out, Mama slowly walked home in the twilight. A beggar asked her for money, and she managed to answer him while carrying her heavy, sleeping child. *"Sarry, me don't hav any money."* The beggar proceeded to curse at her. Mama, in her gentle way, took the time to tell him, still straining under the weight of Josephine. *"Mi no have no money, mi spend the whole day at the hospital because the baby step pon a nail."* She took the time to explain to the man, even while Josephine snuggled into her neck, which was warm and smelled reassuringly, of 'Mama'. Mama always smelled good; even as an older child, Josephine would sit in her mother's lap and sometimes try to put her head under Mama's arms. Mama never pushed her away as a nuisance. She had a compassionate heart towards all people and animals.

The scenes are fleeting for Josephine, born in 1960 and still a baby in 1962 when Jamaica became independent from Britain. Therefore, Carla and Josephine grew up in Kingston, Jamaica, during a time of great cultural transition for Jamaica. New attitudes, values, and empowerment were emerging despite ethnic differences and tensions. At such a young age, Josephine's main focus was her family. Gradually, she became more aware of the extended family and the complicated dynamics that existed because her parents were from two different ethnic groups, East Indian and Afro-Caribbean.

This era in Jamaica saw distinctions among the various ethnic groups widen. The Jamaican whites from many European nations emerged as the people who owned land and still held the wealth after slavery, so they formed the upper class. Chinese and Indian populations were, by nature, merchants and began to thrive in this sector.

The largest part of the population, the people of African descent, were already dealing with the difficult transition to freedom from slavery and now had the added task of dealing with independence from 'The Colonial Motherland,' England. Politics, prejudices and partisanships were further created, and the social classes widened and were cemented along with all the attitudes of superiority, inferiority, oppression and anger. In this macro-sociological 'soup', Josephine and Carla had to learn to function emotionally on the micro level.

Nevertheless, what lingered and stayed as Josephine's focus was the feeling of being a part of a family, a sense of being loved and feeling secure, simple things like the fact that Mama would put her and Carla in similar dresses and shoes. Mama and Papa took evident pride in their offsprings.

Carla was almost three years older than Josephine and had big eyes and long lashes to hide her shyness. Mama told Josephine that when she was a baby, Carla was left alone with her for a few minutes; she took the baby and placed her in a bag as she played. Josephine was unharmed and rather liked being carried along as Carla's toy. As she grew up, Josephine loved Carla and followed her everywhere. The children had a bond that transcended their childhood. They have remained steadfast in each other's lives throughout.

Carla had thick, robust and wavy hair and a light cocoa complexion. Josephine had softer, curly hair and was a bit lighter in hue. Carla was shy, yet she loved to laugh out loud to her heart's content. Although everyone admired her natural beauty and easy disposition, Carla would stay in the background as much as possible. She was happy when people told her how pretty she was, but Josephine saw that her sister was unsure and timid at other times. Josephine was very attuned to how Carla felt and was always ready to defend her as they grew up.

At those times, Carla resorted to cracking her knuckles and looking worried, especially when they visited their East Indian grandmother's home, where their mother's brother, Uncle Keith, lived. The girls thought he was scary because he had piercing black eyes and was very serious with them. Uncle Keith seemed to rule his mother and siblings in their family according to East Indian tradition. He was responsible for the household as he was the senior son. The children also knew he did not like their father because he was not East Indian.

Generally, the East Indian side of the family was not receptive to Josephine's father, and Mama did not help because she, too, seemed to have prejudices against him. Mama would give Papa *'looks'* and make comments that suggested her annoyance and disapproval. This behaviour made the girls' situation confusing for them. As a result of their mixed ethnicity, neither was ever comfortable when they were with either side of their parents' families. Both sides of the family constantly compared the children.

The East Indian family was large: Jestina, Josephine's grandmother and her ten children from two marriages. Jestina was born in 1911 to parents who came from India. Josephine admired her grandmother's grace and poise. She hardly spoke or laughed, and it was evident by her lack of anticipation and joy that she had encountered many hardships in life. Jestina's general resignation to situations spoke of a deeper understanding of life. She had survived two arranged marriages, and when Josephine was old enough to understand, she realised that both had left her grandmother disillusioned with relationships.

What was also evident to Josephine as she grew older was that her grandmother was brilliant with mathematics. Without formal education, she would easily mentally convert the US currency to British sterling and then into Jamaican dollars. Her English was not good due to lack of schooling and being around people who spoke Hindi, but Josephine found it charming as her pronouns never matched up to the gender she was referring to. She would be right at home in the gender confusion of our present time. Josephine concluded that if Jestina had been a woman of her children's or grandchildren's era, she would have been a force to be reckoned with in business or commerce.

Granny Mum was what the girls called Jestina. They were mindful of her as she had eyes that saw everything but kept it all to herself. So schooled was she that after escaping the authority of two husbands, Indian society saw that she became subject to her senior son. A role well played by her, and it was later in life that Josephine persuaded her to share her feelings. On a few occasions, Josephine travelled with *Granny Mum* to the USA to visit her daughters, and they had special sharing and bonding times. Josephine admired that her grandmother's lot did not diminish her integrity, honour, or sense of right and wrong. She remained quietly strong. Like most mothers, she was courageous and only wanted the best for her children. She had Josephine's full respect.

Among her mother's siblings, Josephine had "An Angel." You will meet him too. Uncle John was his name, and he truly seemed to be without guile. In Uncle John's presence, all cares of the world fell away. He had many stray cats that he fed daily. After he died, they all disappeared. There were five aunts and four uncles. Each person made strong impressions on young Josephine, mostly positive ones. Her family was still important to her, but they were all struggling to navigate through the complexities of family dynamics and Indian society. They were encouraged to stay true to their Indian heritage and not to conform too much to western societal expectations. The constant struggle to not fit in was incredibly difficult and resulted in family feuds about relationships, values, etc. Family members whispered rather than discussed issues openly and even hid behaviours they presumed would be frowned upon.

Josephine experienced many Indian-style dinners, festivities and food. The sights and sounds were interesting to Josephine. Still, she was never too engaged as, even though she loved the foods, especially how her grandmother made Roti, the music was not a sound she savoured, as it was usually too high pitched and the voices nasal. She found Indian culture overwhelming to her senses.

'Senior Son,' Uncle Keith, (you will see more of him), excelled in what his Indian grandfather taught him. He was in charge, and his authority was absolute. The girls quaked with fear when they had to visit their grandmother. Uncle Keith would ask the girls, "What nation are you?" He had instructed Josephine to respond, *"Mi a Coolie Uncle Keith"*, and Carla to say, *"Mi a Niega Uncle Keith."* Both terms were derogatory words aimed at belittling the status of an Indian and Negro person. This name-calling made the girls very uncomfortable and insecure among their mother's family. *Maya Angelou once said, "I've learned that people will forget what you said, what you did, but people will never forget how you made them feel."*[1] The feelings of not being good enough were always amplified when the girls visited their Mama's family for one reason or another.

Her parents related stories of their early beginnings. Josephine could not help but feel sad for them because of the potential that they each seemed to have lost. Josephine, her sister, and Papa were Mama's second family, having been married to an East Indian man in the East Indian tradition at age 16. Mama's brother, Uncle Keith, said, "Tin Tin had the biggest wedding event of the year." He further lamented, "We held it at the Muschetts' home on Espeut Avenue, and we spared no money." "Kenneth was paid a dowry, and 'im squander it." The dowry included a shop and land, none of which Mama took with her when she left him. Mama and Kenneth's union produced four children, but it did not last, and Mama did not speak of it much. Josephine knew Mama was sad about her four other children. Later in life, Josephine met her half-siblings and became very close with one brother, who eventually came to stay with them.

Josephine recalls hearing the latch on the gate at the tenement yard where they lived on Payne Avenue, scrape and clang and looking up to see a young man smiling at her. Her mother also saw him, and they were happy to see each other. Tony was his name. He was short and small in body, with Indian hair, bright, smiling eyes, and white teeth. Tony was eleven years older than Josephine and kind, jovial, and happy. To Josephine, Tony seemed to live in a world he alone inhabited. He was a *'know it all'* who liked talking to others as if he knew the facts of any issue.

Tony was also a dreamer who lived his life expecting that at any moment, his 'ship would come in' and he would get rich. His lifelong greetings to Josephine and others was, "*Wey yu a sey?*" This expression was hello to him. His big personality made everyone around him listen to what he had to say. Tony attended Kingston College High School but was expelled in third form. Josephine found it hilarious that all his followers thought he had graduated high school with ten O'Levels. That's how much sway he had over others. Josephine felt that Tony had a big imagination like she did, and even though she loved him, she did not always believe what he said.

He once trained to be a Jockey and fell from a horse, and people said it was responsible for making him a bit 'mad'. Mad meant mentally ill; Josephine did not think Tony was mad, only that he quickly became angry if you disagreed with him. She remembers him fondly as he was caring and nurturing to his two little half-sisters, Carla and herself. When Josephine grew up, she adopted Tony's son and raised him as her son. A smoker for all his adult life, Tony died in 2016 after a long illness of Emphysema. His hopes and anticipation for life were high, up to the moments before he died.

On her father's side, according to Josephine's mother, "Dem sey you a no Alty pickney, yu a jacket." This criticism made her mother very angry with her father's family for the rest of her life. Josephine loved her father and did not believe that he was not her Papa, but based on what her mother accused his family of, Josephine thought that her grandfather, her aunts and her older half-sister did not care much for her. Josephine thought that they only tolerated her.

Papa was the eldest of five children; his mother, Ida May McCalla, was born in 1900 to William James McCalla and Rosella E McCalla. She was one of about eight children. Papa's grandfather reportedly said, "*De* only *tings* black I want on my farm," which was in the hills of St Catherine, "is *mi* hogs." Papa's mother, Ida McCalla, died at 42 years of age, leaving her Afro-Caribbean common-law husband, Novar McDonald, Josephine's paternal grandfather, to raise their five children on his own.

He moved his family back to his people in the parish of Hanover as he and his children did not meet the criteria set out by Papa's grandfather. Not much information is available about Novar McDonald. Josephine remembers him as very stoic, a gentleman who spent his final years helping his daughter Eula maintain her house by cooking and managing until he died of a stroke in 1977. Taken snapshot by snapshot, the emotional dysfunction on both sides of Josephine's family would have provided material for the **Oprah Winfrey** and **Dr Phil** shows, among other long-running talk shows of the 1980s to 2000s, for many seasons.

Notwithstanding, Papa did well in school and was very proud to report, "I was the only boy from my district of Lucea, Hanover, to pass the *Senior Cambridge Examination* the year I sat it." The year was around 1945, and he was full of potential and promise as he was sent to board in Kingston for high school. He eventually joined the *Jamaica Constabulary Force*. Started in 1832 as the permanent policing agency in Jamaica, the force in late 1940 was still under British rule, with all the British standards and values.

Papa had fathered a daughter in Hanover in his early twenties. He related to Josephine what he thought derailed his potential. "Aunt Pearly was a piece of work," He said. Aunt Pearly was his daughter's maternal aunt. Still angry after so many decades, he said, "She sent a letter to the Commissioner of Police, complaining that I was not supporting my child in the country."

"The Commissioner called me in and told me I had two choices: resign or they would fire me; I resigned." He felt robbed of his potential and opportunity at a very young age. Josephine felt helplessly angry on Papa's behalf.

By the time Josephine knew Papa, he had lost all his promised lustre and would spend a large part of his life trying to get sober and keep a job. At first, Josephine was angry with him; she recalls walking down the street one day, holding his hand and asking him, "Why do you sometimes drink Papa, and not at other times?" He just said, "I don't know." Over time, after he would say what he thought had happened to him, Josephine experienced regret for his situation.

Papa spent the last 30 years of his life in a stable job and grew into old age as a distinguished older man. Ironically, at his last job, Papa got to know another man who was also the only boy to pass his *Senior Cambridge Examination* in his district in the same year. This boy, however, became the principal at the college where Papa spent many years working in the printery. The men bonded, Papa and his boss, **Dr Alfred Sangster.** Papa enjoyed knowing that he, too, had started well.

Carla and Josephine grew up together, looking out for each other, which remains to this day. Regardless of what they experienced growing up, they never lost their bond of sisterhood. At around age 13, Mama and Papa sent Carla to live with Papa's sister, Aunt Eula. By then, Aunt Eula, a nurse, had moved her family to Pembroke Hall. Josephine missed her terribly. No one discussed the reason with Josephine, but rather, through overhearing conversations, Josephine gleaned that Carla was having a hard time dealing with Papa's drinking. Left alone with her parents, Josephine became their caregiver.

By the time Josephine was about ten, the family had moved from the tenement yard to another property with units in the yard and an upstairs apartment at 160 Spanish Town Road. Their rooms upstairs were among a dentist's office, a tailor shop and another family, Miss Lyn and *Maas* Aaron and their son Andre`. Josephine still laughs when she recalls the first time she saw the name Andre` written down and realised that the family had mispronounced the little boy's name. He grew up answering to *Andry*.

Still in primary school, Josephine could tell Andre` how to pronounce his name correctly. Josephine liked Miss Lyn but did not feel comfortable pointing it out to her for fear of embarrassing her. She did, however, marvel at the notion that names are used in Jamaica without the proper pronunciation and that most people are proud of their given names; Eugene, a friend of Josephine at school, was called *U-jenny*. Another friend was named Imogene, but the common pronunciation was *I-mo-jean*. She thought, *boy, oh boy, there is a big difference between school English and Jamaican Patwah.*

Miss Lyn was a lovely woman; she was hearing-impaired, very light in complexion and worked away from home. Her husband was quite tall, dark-skinned and had a large head. The men in the dentist's office and the tailor shop on the premises secretly called him names because of his head and wondered among themselves how he managed to get Miss Lyn to marry him. For her part, she told Mama, "Miss Tin-Tin, I don't care what people *sey,* Aaron *tek gud* care of *mi."* Josephine watched Miss Lyn take good care of her family, cooking and cleaning while working away from home and showing her husband *'much respect.'* After living close to each other for years, Josephine lost touch with them when they migrated.

Tony would occasionally visit during this period, but Josephine was mainly alone. As an adult, she now marvels that God's grace protected her as her community looked out for her rather than taking advantage of the vulnerable little girl she must have been. She had no discomfort or fears; she was just lonely. Mama worked long hours to provide for the family, so Josephine cooked, cleaned, and paid the bills. Mama would give her a weekly wage of $9.00 per week, and she would pay the bills that the money could cover and buy the groceries. Papa would be missing most of the time, 'playing dominoes' or drinking until he came home, 'on his face'. There were times that Josephine had to go and fetch him and bring him home. This period of looking after Papa lasted about eight years, spanning late primary school and Josephine's high school years.

Always trying to think ahead, Josephine decided one day when she was about 12 years old to meet Papa at his job on Cargill Avenue in *Half Way Three* on payday. He was working (at one of the many jobs over the years) as a security guard and usually did not have any cash on him by the time he would get home. Arriving on time while all the men were still collecting their pay, Josephine was conspicuous with her long ponytail, socks up to her knees, and pretty dress. She spotted Papa, who was already drunk! He had used up most of his money or had to repay money borrowed, so it was an unsuccessful attempt by Josephine to collect any money from him. The occasion has stayed with Josephine throughout her life for the following reasons.

As they travelled home together on the bus, he had a hard time keeping his balance due to being intoxicated. Josephine placed him on the side seat where the conductor usually sits, but as the bus went around corners, Papa fell off the seat. Josephine helped him up each time to sit back on the seat. Papa smelled of the rum mingled with the Jamaican heat, and the crowded bus smelled sweaty; other passengers started questioning Josephine, "Little girl, *is yu fada dat?*" "Little girl, *is dat* really *yu fada?*" The disbelief on their faces was hard to ignore. Each time, Josephine simply said, "Yes, he is." Getting him home that day was difficult, but

Josephine was glad she could 'own' him and not feel ashamed. She saw the humour, too, as he would steady himself now and then and ask her, "You alright?" "Yes, Papa, hold on," she would say. The smell of alcohol on any man is still a powerful negative trigger for Josephine, as the memories of having to deal with Papa at those times never diminish.

During this period, Josephine, once again walking to take a bus with Papa, realised that something was happening, as he was complaining about people speaking badly about him, and they were the only two together. Josephine told her Aunt Eula what was happening, and Aunt Eula advised her to take Papa to Dr Audley Betton on Manning Hills Road. It seems Papa was having a nervous breakdown. It happened twice, and each time, Josephine had to take charge. She took him for his injections, travelled home with him on the bus while he was falling asleep and would get him home safely. Josephine never paused to gauge her feelings too much; she did what she had to do.

Thankfully, he recovered, but it would still be many years before he would slowly stop drinking enough to function normally and keep a job. All of this happened in the 1970s and coincided with the period in Jamaica when there were food shortages of rice, flour and other basic commodities. Josephine had a good relationship with Miss Beryl's family (from the tenement yard), who had a grocery store. She would shop for groceries weekly, and Miss Beryl's brother Nim would ensure she could get rice and flour that all grocery stores rationed.

Under the **Michael Manley administration in the 1970s**, Jamaica went through a period of austerity as the government embarked on strict policies to improve the country's fiscal situation. The government restricted the importation of goods and services, resulting in severe food shortages. The program was designed to encourage more local production, thus resulting in less use of foreign exchange. Miss Beryl's mother, Miss Jenny and other women affirmed Josephine as they saw her managing her parents' household and carrying the adult responsibilities.

Mama, for her part, never stopped working. She found the weekly bus fare and lunch money for Carla, who came to collect it on Sunday evenings. Josephine lived for Sundays when Carla would visit accompanied by their cousin Cher, whom Josephine loves and whom you will meet in the story Blessed Weevil Peas. Over time, Josephine also had a visiting relationship with Aunt Eula and her family. She could not live with them permanently, but she was allowed to stay overnight sometimes.

Josephine's parents were only separated by death when Mama died in Oct 1998 at the age of 72 after about 44 years together. Papa, who had only just retired from his job at the college printery, was devastated. He was lost as they had started functioning with some normalcy later in life. They were both enjoying companionship, watching television together, discussing politics and looking out for Josephine and Carla to visit with their children. Papa spent the rest of his life living between his daughters and their families in Canada and Jamaica, passing away in September 2011 at the age of 82. He was a beloved father and grandfather.

Eventually, Josephine and Carla came to enjoy the privilege of being recognised as valuable to both sides of their families. Whenever an occasion arises to visit with family, they are warmly welcomed, with genuine affection and appreciation. There are deep wells of love on both sides of Josephine's family for Josephine and Carla. A trip to any of her aunts in America usually results in an impromptu family reunion and big pots of stew peas and rice. Together, they reminisce about the good times and can share even the hardships they experienced and how they triumphed over adversities.

Josephine believes that her family is one of many whose experiences are similar. Starting humbly, learning each day by the grace of God to survive, managing meagre provisions, and dealing well with emotional issues until they start to function better, all the while having hope that better will come for the next generation.

It's typical how Jamaica evolved as a multicultural society showcasing an actual 'Melting Pot' of cultures, values, and faiths: Tainos, West Africans, East Indians, Chinese, South East Asians, Jews, Syrians, Lebanese, and Europeans - [Spanish, French, German and Scandinavian] and British - [English, Irish, Scottish, and Welsh]. It made sense to Josephine that the motto of her beloved Jamaica is, **Out of Many, One People.** Every time she said the National Pledge in school at morning assembly or sang the National Anthem standing at attention, she looked up at her flag being hoisted with pride. Her family exemplified this reality of becoming one as they realised they were stronger together than apart.

Glossary

Acolyte - A person assisting the celebrant in a religious service or procession.

A jacket - paternity fraud

Estate - An extensive area of land used for farming etc. Particularly during slavery and indentured servitude, workers on the land, resided on the land during their contract period.

Coolie - A coolie was an indentured East Indian Labourer. The term originated among the British Bureaucrats in Colonial India and followed suit in Jamaica. It was a derogatory word when used by locals on the island.

Dr Alfred Sangster - Retired President of The University of Technology, formerly College of Art, Science and Technology.

Half Way Tree - A main shopping and commercial area in Kingston Jamaica. Formerly was the imaginary line between 'uptown and downtown'.

Niega - Derived from the Latin Negro- meaning Black. It was a derogatory term for Africans living on the Island.

On his face - drunk and barely conscious.

Overseer - A supervisor, often in the agricultural industry, managing farms, livestock and workers.

Ship would come in - waiting for wealth or success.

Standpipe - A vertical pipe extending from a main water supply, especially one connecting a temporary tap to the main. Usually found in communities where there are no formal residences, and amenities are communal.

Taino - An indigenous tribe of the Arawak people formerly inhabiting Jamaica, among other Greater Antilles Islands and the Bahamas.

Third form - 9th grade

End Note
[1] This excerpt is from the Maya Angelou Film- And Still I Rise. 2016 https://www.imdb.com/title/tt5142750

THE
PROMENADE

In 1966, Josephine was six years old. Her yard had a wide frontage onto Spanish Town Road, a major thoroughfare to this day. The road was very long and extended from downtown Kingston to Spanish Town, the old capital. Divided into segments designated by miles, she lived at *Three Miles*, where she eventually attended school.

Josephine felt that her world was vast. It was too big for a little girl as she experienced situations that, taken literally, were scary, overwhelming and hard to understand. The unknown to a child was daunting and often filled with imagined perils. Josephine imagined that:

The bus may nuh stop where me want it tu. Suppose me nuh tall enough fi reach de bell tu ring it, to get de bus dri-va fi stop, den de bus a go carry me wey?

The road was too wide to get across on her own safely. What if it rained? How would she cross the swift running water on the streets? What if the adults were mean and cruel? The scenarios were many and varied; however, as she grew up and discovered the other areas, her sense of ease grew.

There was *Two Miles*, which housed a busy market, where the ground was black from the charcoal sold there. Josephine felt dirty in the market on the black ground. Close to the market were two landmarks that she remembered for very different reasons; the first was the unpaved lane, Norman Lane, where her grandmother lived halfway up, and the entrance from which the market fanned out. The second reason is that there was a **Bata Shoes** store right beside the market. The white sneakers, beautiful loafers, and other 'church' shoes displayed in its windows contrasted with the black ground of the market. Like other children, Josephine no doubt viewed the beautiful, clean, new shoes in the shop window and wished she would receive a pair at Christmas.

Two Miles lost its mystery and scariness as she visited her grandmother increasingly and became used to the area. However, she still had many other areas to discover, disquietingly so to her. She tried to imagine what *Four Miles* and *Five Miles* may look like.

Eventually, she discovered some of the 'far away places', such as *Four Miles*, as Papa worked at a paper factory called Paper Processors Ltd in that area. She and her sister travelled on the Jamaica Omnibus Service, JOS, on some Sundays to take his dinner when he had to work overtime. At first, this was daunting for Josephine as the bus took them into uncharted territories. Over time, the excursions became something to look forward to rather than be afraid of. They enjoyed being responsible for delivering his dinner in a *'carrier'* made of three enamel containers that fitted neatly on each other. The containers were held in place by two metal braces on either side of the stack of containers. Each container held meat, rice, yams, bananas, and salad. The metal brace reminded Josephine of the iron brace children suffering from Polio had to wear.

The girls also enjoyed being admired by Papa's co-workers, who thought they were beautiful children and said so every time they saw them. Josephine recalls enjoying that her dad would always seem happy at the admiration of his children.

When she went to school in 1966, the little observer discovered *Three Miles* even better and became more comfortable with her world. 'Back To' was an area that many of her school friends lived in. At *'Back To,'* a fresh-food market came alive between Thursdays and

Saturdays. Vendors travelled on buses and trucks with every type of ground provision, fruit, vegetable, and meat imaginable. On those market days, life became much more dynamic as vendors conducted business, acquaintances were renewed from the week before, and fellow shoppers shared commentaries about the latest on Jamaican life in vivid Jamaican parlance. 'Mind yu step pon mi singting' a vendor would caution someone walking too close to her tomatoes. "Lawd the pumpkin pretty dis week sah." Another would observe. "Di yam dem soft dis week?" Asked another. "Rain wash out di lettuce," lamented someone else.

As Josephine got older, she did get a chance to traverse the entire route of Spanish Town Road, demystifying her sense that it was a really long road that led to parts of Kingston that she could only imagine and held stranger things than she knew. It turned out that it was just another section of the same road with people having the exact needs and going about meeting those needs. What she experienced from her vantage point in her yard was just a slice of the same life happening along the road.

All major processions passed by their yard over the years. Funerals, festivals, parades, political campaigning convoys and visiting foreign officials. Cars drove by daily with different types of people. To Josephine, the differences were not evident; they were only strangers who operated motorcars. The opinions of the adults around her couldn't have been more confusing to Josephine as they seemed to see a clear distinction between the people driving by and themselves. For example, a car passing by may be carrying 'oppressors', those perpetuating colonialism, or just simply rich people who were 'obviously' not good people because they are rich.

Josephine recalls *'looking out'* early one morning, and a car stopped to allow a female passenger to open the door and 'be sick' several times. She naturally recognised that the woman was feeling unwell and felt sorry for her, inside of her head, of course. That's when she heard Slim Lloydy's commentary on the issue; people described him as so black that only his eyes were visible at night. He shouted curse words, "**$%&** Is all the rich food that dem **$%&** *people eat, mek dem cum down ya a sick soh.*" As you can imagine, Josephine was puzzled for many years. She guessed he assumed that if you were able to operate a motor vehicle, then you were rich, and if you were rich, you should be denied sympathy even if you were feeling unwell.

Fortunately, Josephine grew in knowledge and understanding and often wondered how sad it must be to see life through such an opaque lens. She watched him for many years; unfortunately, no learning or better understanding of human circumstances seemed to have stuck to him. Not all of her observations were negative; some were scary, and others were beyond her understanding of their significance at the time.

From these early beginnings, Josephine first saw a **Junkanoo Band**, men dressed up in costumes dancing to the music of a **Mento Band** in a procession down the street. Mento is a style of Jamaican folk music recognisable by its acoustic sounds. Drums, Banjo, Gourd Shakers, Maracas, and other metal percussion instruments make up the sound. It is a fusion of African and Irish Rhythms that are lively and upbeat. The *Junkanoo bands* appeared at Christmas and New Year. The parade generated much excitement as the dancers tried to stir the crowd into frenzied merriment. The *ScareCrow*, *Pitchi-Patchi*, the *Devil* and the *Belly Woman were among the most popular characters.*

As you may already surmise, the experience was traumatic for a 6-year-old. The dancers also collected money along the way. The combination of a scared child, running and crying, and the need to encourage the crowd to drop coins into their buckets sometimes was enough to have a dancer work overtime in one location. While most adults laughed, mothers would half-heartedly try to reassure the children that the parade and the characters in the parade were all harmless. *The Devil* had a pitch-fork and horns on his head; *Pitchi-Patchi* had no representation in life that a child could relate to, as the costume was made up of hundreds of pieces of colourful cloth, all tattered and torn; the *ScareCrow* was not worldly to look at, and *Belly Woman* was able to move her 'belly' in ways that a child had never seen before. The facial masks all had leering, wide grins and evil eyes. To a child, this was a nightmare or the making of one. Thankfully, for Josephine, this tradition seems to have diminished over time.

In keeping with grotesque memories, Josephine remembers a fat politician who came campaigning riding on a horse. She recalls his name very well; those around her said it. Those were also the days when children had to recite the National Pledge, remember acronyms and synonyms and the names of government ministers, etc. Remaining nameless in this story, he was, at the time, Minister of Housing. What a spectacle that was as his supporters came out to greet him. Josephine, however, was upset as her sympathy was for the poor horse bearing such a heavy burden. "Watch 'ow 'im *belly heng over de horse,*" said a spectator. "*'Im shudda* carry *de* horse." Said someone else. "*Dat* is so unfair to *de* horse; it *caa'n* manage such a burden," was another comment.

The minister was pleased as he greeted his constituents from atop his horse. He may have thought he looked regal on his horse, but the horse was the one that looked impressive. The minister looked dishevelled, untidy and sweaty, while the horse was sleek and powerful, trotting along as if dancing. Suddenly, the magnificent beast reared up on its hind legs gave out a high '*whi-iiiny*' and took off running because of the crush of the crowd and the sound of a shrill car horn that was sounded to disperse the crowd walking before the minister. The horse was startled, bucked, reared, and the minister crouched low and forward, holding on for dear life, as the horse ran through the scattered crowd. The sound of the horse's whinnying was enough to indicate the abuse it was feeling from the heavy minister and the surging crowd.

Thankfully for the minister, there were mounted police personnel riding on the sidelines, and they could catch up with the bolted animal and calm its jitters. The minister was able to dismount, mopping his face and hobbling to the prepared platform, where he tried to use humour to regain his equilibrium before he gave his speech. The audience laughed with him and even congratulated him on his quick show of expert horsemanship, of course. The show continued with speeches and and the crowd's shouts of agreement as the moment's politics played out.

On Sundays, Josephine could identify hearses before she could count numbers correctly. These long black cars led the procession of other cars going east along Spanish Town Road to the *May Pen Cemetery*. Josephine knew that each procession was a funeral and each coffin carried a dead body. Her understanding of these events was gleaned from the various commentaries from the adults around her. Inevitably, seeing a hearse would remind a patron at the shop, managed by her mother, of a recent death. The subject would be discussed in living colour and Jamaican parlance. *"Maas So and So"* or *"Miss So and So"*, son, daughter, *pickney, relative did drownded"*, *"Car lick im down"*, or *"Mi did get a dream sey, sup'em bad ago 'appen, an it go soh."* On and on, she heard of the many and varied ways that people could die.

The Pantomime reached its climax by afternoon when the rum bar opened. Drunken men entertained each other about friends they had lost. The rum in their stomachs and glasses made each story larger than life. So, a sudden death, even if it was by natural causes, took on sinister tones; maybe a little *Obeah* was added, or maybe a vengeful God was disappointed because the deceased had gone to church and was convicted to accept the Lord and left without doing so. No death was without an omen or superstition. The stories flowed as long as the hearses passed on the outside road.

Where was Josephine? She would typically be behind the counter between the shop and the bar; she sometimes sipped a **Pepsi** or ate bun and cheese, a staple for her and her sister in those days. Or she would be playing outside the shop and bar front, on the piazza. Meanwhile, on the outside, the music was easier on her ears. Inside, the Jukebox was too loud.

Some songs made Josephine sad, such as **Walk On By by Dionne Warwick.** Especially on Sundays, it seemed that out of reverence, it being The Lord's Day, the songs selected on the JukeBox were hauntingly sad. **Skeeter Davis's- Am I That Easy to Forget**; **Jim Reeves, Take My Hand, Precious Lord, This World is Not My Home, etc....** Josephine liked **Sam Cooke** because Papa would snap his fingers and sing along with the *Jukebox* to his songs. That engendered good feelings, but others were unhappy, and being a child, she interpreted the words literally, so she wondered, for example, where Jim Reeves thought his home was.

To this day, listening to the radio on Sundays can bring back feelings of melancholy for Josephine. The only reprieve on such Sunday evenings after hearing about deaths, watching funeral processions, and listening to the soundtrack of sad love songs was the happy sound of the ice cream man. She heard his bicycle bell's familiar 'Tingaling, Tingaling'. Sometimes, she was lucky enough to get an ice cream cone. Those were glorious Sunday afternoons.

As Josephine grew up, her understanding and appreciation for the things happening around her allowed her to relax and enjoy her 'runway' to life. When she experienced Jamaica's early Independence Day celebrations, decorated floats would pass outside her yard. The country had a show called the *Grand Gala* to celebrate the culmination of various events over the days leading up to Independence Day on August 6th. There were street dances, festival songs and drama competitions, and the relatively new Jamaican flag flew everywhere. The gas station across the street would be decorated with triangle-shaped bunting and flags of bold black, vibrant green and golden yellow. People would be dressed in the designated colour for the festival season, sometimes down to a specific fabric.

In this festive atmosphere, she would watch from the piazza of the shop and bar decorated trucks carrying national beauty queens, parish queens, and winners of various regional competitions. The trucks would have music blaring, and the beauty queens would wave at those on the sidelines and throw candies to the onlookers. Josephine was too young to scramble for the sweets but still enjoyed the show. She later understood that these floats meandered through the neighbourhoods in and around Kingston before making their way to the National Stadium for the *Grand Gala* show, which began in 1963.

Back in the 1960s, Jamaica was still composed of a few undiluted ethnicities, each trying to maintain its traditions – the *Chinese New Year* was celebrated differently from everybody else. The celebrations occurred between the end of January and the end of February, depending on the new moon's arrival. Josephine became aware of these celebrations because of the many Chinese-owned bakeries and grocery stores along Spanish Town Road. Arising from rich Chinese traditions of thousands of years ago, the lunar festivals include lights, fireworks, red lanterns and garments and the making of giant red dragons. Families celebrate with music and feastings.

The East Indians also had their festivals. Some, such as the *Hosay*, were Muslim in origin. They were celebrated in August to commemorate the martyrdom of the Prophet Mohammad's grandsons Hassan and Hussein at the battle of Kerbala, Persia. The festivities lasted several days and took the form of a street procession; the celebrants carried decorated models of mosques and waved colourful flags. Drummers also accompanied the celebrants.

As a child, a parade was a parade, and there was no understanding of any more considerable religious significance. The Hindus commemorated the festival of lights in November, called *Diwali*, symbolising the victory of light over darkness. They, too, would decorate their businesses and homes with lights, exchanging gifts, fireworks, puja (prayers), and family gatherings, enjoying music and feasting.

Josephine remembers vividly experiencing two other grand events as the parades passed outside her house: the motorcade of two monarchs in 1966. The first was of **Emperor Haile Selassie**, who attracted hundreds of

Rasta men outside her fence and gate as they lined the procession route along the Spanish Town Road; they occupied every tree and any elevated space requiring a climb for access.

Rastafarianism is a religious sect in Jamaica that was in its early genesis observing the Ethiopian Emperor as a direct descendant from the line of King David of the Bible. They hailed him as the expected Messiah. Their dress, personal deportment, i.e. uncut 'hair-locks' and vegetarian diet called 'Ital food', are edicts taken from the Old Testament. They presume themselves to be from the historical twelve tribes of Israel.

Josephine cannot recall ever noticing a *Rasta* man before this time. So she was fascinated by their clothes; some wore Khaki outfits like those you see on hunters in the jungle. They adorned their shirts with different emblems and brooches. Others had long white robes. They all had growths of matted hair of varying lengths, of which they seemed incredibly proud.

They carried walking sticks or staff and spent time waiting, singing, drumming and chanting. They even seemed to be speaking a different language, as they used the word "I and I" multiple times in reference to themselves.

They waited patiently for one day in the Jamaican sun, and the Emperor did not drive by. On the second day, they appeared again and were rewarded with a brief glimpse of him as his car drove by. Josephine can't recall any impression of the Emperor, but his followers certainly left an indelible mark on her consciousness at the time.

Then, the British Monarch **Queen Elizabeth 11** and her husband, **Prince Phillip,** were also driven along the route, passing by Josephine's gate. On that occasion, however, people were more formally dressed. Hats were still in vogue for both men and women. Some women even wore gloves. Girls wore ribbons in their hair, socks pulled up to their knees, and crinolines under their skirts. The crowd was more timid than the Rastafarians as they stood single file, waiting to glimpse the Queen and to see her wave as a passing greeting. Seeing her reminded Josephine of the few times she had seen black and white television. It was as if she had stepped into a *newsreel.*

The observations of the two sets of spectators of both monarchs spoke volumes to Josephine about the old Jamaica and the newly emerging Jamaica. Jamaicans were transformed in how they dressed, talked, conducted themselves and decided what was necessary. The promenade of Jamaican life that passed by her yard left a deep impression on Josephine. She realised her good fortune at witnessing, at such an early age, her country in transition. She realised that the people around her were learning to become independent Jamaicans, no longer British citizens.

Jamaica still had many of the trappings of colonialism; the bus service, its British way of dressing, expressions, using titles such as Mr,

Mrs, Miss, Master or Maas, etc. People's sensibilities were still very British even though the Jamaican way was rapidly emerging, where people were saying what they felt and were taking no prisoners. Josephine is grateful for the exposure to the variety and multi-faceted character of Jamaican life that her childhood offered her. It has undoubtedly placed her in a unique position of understanding and relating to people of different circumstances with respect and courtesy.

Jamaicans are genuinely, **Out of Many One People,** Josephine thought to herself. She had a front-row seat to watch this national motto play out. Looking back, Josephine realised that as varied as Jamaicans are, their differences are mostly 'skin-deep' and mainly status-defined. Jamaica is blessed as a nation with the natural beauty of its mountains, rivers, and beaches and blessed with people who have strong convictions of the sovereignty of their Creator and the loving-kindness of their Saviour.

All were displayed before Josephine as a child as she observed the colourful parade of people passing along life's promenade.

Glossary

Bata Shoes Stores - An early shoe store chain, Bata originated in 1894 in Czechoslovakia. In 1939, Bata moved the Store's headquarters to Ontario, Canada, and thereafter, in the early 1930s, it supplied shoes to Jamaica and Trinidad.

It was a family-owned business that provided trendy shoes at affordable prices and friendly staff. The stores were known for their welcoming aroma of leather, rubber and suede and were a staple for footwear in Jamaica. Famous footwear items were Jelly's, rubber sandals, flip flops, rubber slippers, soft walk shoes, an early version of trainers, and leather shoes for school and formal wear.

By 1938, there were 12 stores on the island of Jamaica. Owning shoes from a Bata store was prestigious for the underprivileged as being waited on and fitted with your size was novel treatment for the poorer classes who, before then, went to local cobblers to buy shoes.

Stores stayed in operation on the Island until 1985.

Source;

- Jaroslav Pospíšil — Hana Pospíšilová, Rub a líc baťovských sporů, Zlín 2012, ISBN 978-80-7473-037-5
- Thomas J. Bata, Remembered, Zlín 2016, ISBN 978-80-7473-398-7
- Moravský zemský archiv v Brně — Státní
- okresni archiv Zlin ,Cesko

Edwin L Martin , Montserrat Spotlight, February 20, 2022

Church Shoes - Jamaican term for formal shoes, not worn to school or for play.

Crinoline - is a stiff fabric made of horsehair and cotton or linen thread, used for stiffening petticoats or as a lining under ladies dresses or skirts.

Obeah - is a kind of sorcery/witchcraft
practised primarily in the Caribbean.

THE
TENEMENT
YAAD

*G*rowing up in Kingston, Jamaica, in the early 1960s, carefree and innocent Josephine's world was as big as her imagination, "It was this big, and it *run mi* down fast, fast, fast", she said to Mama, holding her little arms as far apart as she could, showing Mama the size of a cow she had seen.

Her big imagination allowed her to often entertain herself with whatever discarded household item she could find. An empty cardboard box could quickly become a doll's house. The back legs of an old seatless chair, used for seating under the shady mango tree, could create lanes for make-believe cars by running the legs along the dirt.

Josephine enjoyed playing by imagining situations into existence. She thought *Christopher Columbus* must have been a giant to have discovered the world. *Wonda if him wi step pon me?* Similarly, she thought that *Ole` Appleseed John* must have had a belly ache because he had to eat so many apples before he could plant the seeds. These were wonderful times for Josephine; she had heard many stories and had a treasure trove of ideas to make-believe. So Josephine spent many happy hours playing by herself.

Aside from Josephine, her family consisted of Mama, also known as *Tin-Tin and* Papa, called Alty. Josephine also had an older sister named Carla. Josephine's family was not unlike many Jamaican families. Mixed in ethnicity between East Indians on her mother's side and Afro Caribbean with Scottish or Irish influences, they were well and truly 'mutts'. Her parents were unmarried, possibly because her mother was previously married and was still married and also because she decided not to get married a second time. *"Mi married one time already at Kingston Parish Church, mi naa do it again,"* Mama would say whenever the topic came up. She had four children within her marriage with her estranged husband, who had custody of them and, therefore, raised them. On the other hand, Papa had never been married but had an older daughter from his late teenage years. Josephine and Carla were never totally comfortable with either side of their family as the 1960s and 1970s in Jamaica were still steeped in prejudices of ethnicity, social status and generalised tensions of an emerging independent nation.

The children lived with their family in a *tenement yaad*, a big compound with multiple houses. Josephine's family was among eight tenants who paid rent to the landlord, who did not reside on the premises. Notably, Miss Beryl and her boyfriend, Mr Austin, and her two daughters Joan pronounced in Patwah, *Juwan* and Jeannie and Mr and Mrs Francis and their daughter Janet. Other people moved in and out throughout the time Josephine lived there. The property was large and had various units made of concrete blocks, which were exposed by weathering so that you could see the outline of each brick. The walls were rough, with visible seams between the concrete blocks. The units varied in size from one room to three rooms. The children would use even a unit size as bragging rights among themselves. *"Mii ouse bigga dan fi yu ouse,"* a proud child would say to another.

As Josephine spent time around the adults, she gathered information about the running of the place. "When di landlord need money, *im buil anada* room," they said. It seemed that most units were added haphazardly over time as needed. It appears that rooms were erected on the next-best spot.

All the houses had zinc roofs that leaked when it rained. It was expected to see various pots and pans catching water that leaked into the units from the zinc roofs. Tenants would place a pan or basin under a leak and then shift it around until it was covered. Josephine remembers the sounds of the dripping water—the ping of a small drip and the louder plops of the heavier leaks. The drips and leaks created rhythmic patterns that Josephine could sing out loud while using her fingers to play on an imaginary piano, finding enjoyment even on a rainy day.

Ping, plop, ping ping, plop, ping, plop, ping ping, plop... Ping, plop, ping, ping, plop... went the sounds of the leaks.

After the rain shower, inside the house was cooler and outside there was a fresh scent of wet dirt and the sense that the rain washed everything clean. On hot days, the zinc would seem to be making sighing sounds as it heated up in the Jamaican sunshine. 'Uwaaahhh', said the roof. Added to the actual increase in temperature that this brought, being indoors on those days was not pleasant, as the air inside was hot and stifling. Mould and damp odours would rise when the units became hot inside.

Another feature of the houses was cellars. Spaces under each house were created by placing the units on stilts or blocks. The spaces were high enough for animals like dogs, cats and chickens to hide under or for a small child to crawl around to explore. Over time, these dark cellars held discarded bottles, pans and other garbage items. Josephine feared lizards and spiders, so she rarely ventured into a cellar. In Jamaica, giant, green ground lizards ran around aplenty; to Josephine, these were scary.

The houses each had a faded front door and one or two windows made from wooden frames with cracked and broken planes of glass held in place by caulking that had seen better days and were now cracked and brittle. Tenants used plyboard or cardboard to repair broken windows. The tenants developed this unplanned patchwork of wood and cardboard, as the landlord never replaced the glass panes. Josephine could hear the tenants saying, "*The rent high, and the landlord not fixing anything*", or '*Mi naa* pay *de* rent *cause de plaace waan fi fix.*" The colours of the houses were also very faded, except for a few places that had escaped the sun's rays; it was hard to tell the original colour.

The largest and nicest unit was at the front of the premises. The walls seemed smoother, the paint was bright, and there were no broken panes of glass. Josephine realised as she got older that it was the original structure of the yard, going back to colonial times, when things were grander, and the family who lived there could afford to live in a big detached house. It had a living room, a kitchen, two rooms, and a bathroom facility.

A married couple, Mr. and Mrs. Francis, and their daughter, Janet, also rented this unit. Mr and Mrs Francis and two teachers from primary school became examples for Josephine to live by. Josephine liked this family and enjoyed spending time with them. They were a constant in the yard. They were already living there when Josephine and her family moved in and remained there when Josephine's family moved out. They eventually purchased the property years later.

Usually lost in her imaginings, the characters in the yard seemed to operate on the fringes of Josephine's consciousness, except if she had any direct contact with them. Then, her mind would engage in the situation and seem to record the interactions. Josephine seemed to know without understanding how, who cared for her and who was a 'safe' person that she and Carla could trust. Or she could pinpoint who was a 'news carrier' likely to report on the children's behaviour to their parents.

Josephine thought that the single man who lived in one room at the back of the premises was not to be trusted. He seemed unnaturally neat and clean in appearance and was lighter in complexion. He was often away from home and never joined the community chats under the mango tree. The children only played by his quarters sometimes. On one rare occasion, a group of children were near his door, and he happened to be home, sitting in the doorway. He was engrossed in a magazine with a half-dressed woman on the cover cuddling a cat. Stanley, a younger, curious boy, asked him, "*Whe she get de cat from?*" "You wouldn't understand, but maybe she would," he said. This statement suggested that Stanley was too young to understand how the woman got the cat, but perhaps Josephine would. He further explained. "This is how she got the cat."

Blah, blah, blah... His words went over Josephine's head; contrary to what he had thought, she certainly did not know what he had meant. His storybook was not what she was used to seeing. She never knew his name and couldn't remember when he disappeared; she certainly didn't miss him and thought he was odd.

Some people moved quickly in and out of the yard, while others became neighbours for extended periods. One such transient tenant was 'Miss Willy', a tall, dark man who lived among the tenants briefly with his girlfriend. He had the distinction of being called 'Miss Willy' instead of Mr. Willy. It happened that a little girl among the children could not say, mister, so in an insightful moment, the child, observing a melting block of ice, said quite clearly, "Miss Willy, Miss Willy, *de-ice a pee pee.*" He kept that name until he disappeared from Josephine's view.

Miss Willy wore a mesh undershirt as his outside shirt. He did not seem to have regular work and so had more time to report on the children's behaviour. The children were careful when Miss Willy was around as he 'told on them'. Josephine did not always agree with his account of events and thought that he lied. Once, Josephine pushed Mrs Francis's daughter Janet, and she fell. The children had been playing, and Janet, using her foot, kept erasing Josephine's make-believe house drawn in the dirt. Miss Willy reported the incident to Mr Francis. "*De likkle pikney shub ar so hard she couldn't get up, and she was holding ar chest*", He said. Josephine got a spanking as Mr Francis complained to Papa, explaining that Janet is a sickly child and Josephine could have seriously hurt her. Josephine was not sorry. She had pushed Janet and thought, *Janet a hole ar chest like seh mi push ar hard. Miss Willy is a liad; 'im neva even see wha happen.*

Miss Willy's girlfriend was on her way to being fat as she, along with other women, drank what they called 'pot wata' to get fat. To Jamaicans, pot water was a starchy liquid, resulting from boiled ground provisions such as green banana, yam, or potato. Josephine recalls *Juwan,* Carla's friend and playmate, encouraging her to drink the dark water as Josephine was very skinny. Miss Willy's girlfriend, however, drank it regularly.

Josephine does not recall her name but that she had a bigger-than-usual neck. The children secretly described what appeared to be a breast nipple on her neck as the *'bumping tit-tit'*. As her neck got more prominent, the adults in the yard said, *"She hav goiter an if she nu cut it before it grow big, it caan cut again but she fraid fi cut it."* Josephine gleaned that Miss Willy's girlfriend had thyroid disease that needed immediate medical attention because, after a while, doctors would not be able to treat the growth. Josephine had seen other women before with what looked like a third breast hanging from their neck area and imagined that this was what the adults were talking about. Sitting among her neighbours under the shady mango tree, she wished that "Miss Willy's girlfriend would be brave enough to visit the doctor, as she watched her unconsciously twisting her *'bumping tit-tit.'*

The families consisted of children, single mothers, common-law couples, a single man and one married couple. Miss Venice was one of the single mothers in the Yaad; she had three young children. She was thin, rarely smiled, always sad, and often the subject of other women's gossip. The women would speak with her sympathetically, but behind her back, they were very judgemental of her circumstances and even speculated about her source of income. Josephine was sorry for Miss Venice, who seemed like a nice woman. She did not sit to chat under the mango tree but came in tired from doing her 'Day's Work,' looking worried; she would always say the proper greetings as she passed, but Josephine knew she was unhappy by the look in her eyes.

Once, Miss Venice's father came to stay with her to help with the children. Josephine observed that one day while making bush tea for the baby, he realised that a roach had gotten into the **Betty** Condensed Milk tin. Back then, people opened a milk tin by punching two triangle-shaped holes on opposite sides on top of the can with a can opener. As there were no refrigerators, people either poured the condensed milk into a bottle and fastened it with a lid, or the holes were plugged with paper. To Josephine's horror, Miss Venice's father pulled the roach out and carried on using the milk. As slowly as condensed milk runs out of the can, 'blup, blup, blurp', that's how slowly the roach came out. Josephine knew he had to do it because they couldn't afford to throw away a whole can of milk, but it unsettled her so much that, instantly, her vigilance against roaches was born.

Josephine's family lived in two rooms. They had two beds separated by a curtain and a dresser for storing clothes. The dresser was mainly used to store any garment Josephine's mother deemed 'gud clothes.' Inside the drawers, the clothes were not folded neatly but just stuffed inside to get them out of the way. These were like Sunday school clothes. Mamma washed everyday clothes like uniforms and 'yaad clothes' and placed them on top of a barrel. The rotation of such clothes was too often to pack them away.

Josephine believes that the barrel came from the United States of America a long ago from a relative who had migrated. The barrel's beige colour had, over time, become brown due to age. *The tings in the barrel smell bad. Why is Mama keeping dem?* Josephine thought as she rummaged through the neglected items in the barrel. Inside the barrel, she smelled camphor balls mixed with dampness; the mouldy scent and sight of old things also brought regret that something no longer could fit or be used. A beautiful gold blouse Josephine received from an aunt abroad was a typical example of such a neglected item of clothing. Josephine liked it and tried several times to wear it, but it itched her skin, and she eventually had to leave it alone. Mamma forgot this blouse, among other items, in the barrel.

In the front room, Josephine's family had a dinette set with four chairs, a two-burner gas stove on top of a metal stand and a **Sylvania** television. These items were still a wish for most of Josephine's neighbours. So she enjoyed the sense of empowerment she experienced as the neighbours stood by the window to view the news or a cowboy show on television at night. The other tenants would take their seats outside the door when a particular program was on, like **Nuggets for the Needy** or **Miss Lou and maas Ran Show** with *Louise Bennett and Ranny Williams*. Papa would move the television, sitting on its stand, to face the front door so it could be enjoyed by those sitting outside. On Sunday nights, people would watch musical shows such as **Tom Jones, Cilla Black, and John Davison** on JBC TV. Josephine recalls thinking, *How we buy TV and can't pay the rent?* Josephine did not discuss this television business with anyone else in the yaad but only with the Mango Tree.

There were no kitchens, so each unit had a setup outside where tenants used a coal-burning stove to prepare meals or a gas stove inside the room. The families shared common facilities like a cistern with a 'standpipe' for water, two showers and two toilets. The cistern was big and square and made out of stone. The pipe was high enough from the cistern's floor to allow larger washing pans or buckets to sit under the pipe as users filled up containers with water. Using the cistern was challenging for Josephine and the smaller children as they needed to climb onto the cistern wall to turn the pipe on. She learned early to fetch water to wash the dishes and her socks, uniforms, and underwear. She enjoyed washing her clothes as she revelled in causing her fingers to make high-pitched squishy sounds like the adults. *Scrips, scrips, scrips...* went her fingers as she used laundry soaps such as **Fab** or **Breeze** or bars of **Blue Soap** to wash her clothes.

Leaving the pan to fill on its own would often result in a fuss among the adults, as a pan overflowing would cause a conscious person to lament the waste of the water. What Josephine found difficult was holding the bucket as it filled with water; it was too heavy for her. Added to this, Josephine tried her best not to put her container inside the cistern as it had green, slimy, 'icky' stuff growing on the stone floor. Josephine would precariously fill her bucket to the level she could manage while still holding it. This amount was not a lot of water, but it was the only way to avoid the 'icky' green stuff.

The yard was large and had two gates to the front of the property. Pedestrians gained access by walking through the smaller of two gates that had previously been painted bright green but had faded to a dull, distressed-looking green. The rusted, triangle-shaped, iron metal lock on the gate announced that someone was coming through it as the person entering lifted it. Then, as it fell back into place, the decisive 'screech, clang' sound the latch made would cause Josephine to hurriedly strain her neck to see who was coming into the yard. The more enormous, wider black metal gate was only opened when the landlord came to collect his rent once a month. He would get out of his car, open the gate, drive into the yard and close it behind him. Josephine thought to herself, 'Im important'.

Both gates were faded green, with the more enormous gate having metal slats in a grid pattern that had been meshed long ago but was torn in pieces and rusty by then. There was a front fence made of faded green pickets with nails so rusted and raised that they seemed to create a pattern on the wooden pickets. A careless brush against the fence could result in serious cuts or bruises. This fence separated the property from the sidewalk outside. Interestingly, faded and old as the picket fence was, it was superior to some other yards where fences had broken down over time and were left in various states of disrepair. In those yards, goats, dogs and even cows sometimes wandered in.

Barbed wire fences ran along the neighbouring sides, and a *Common Mango* mango tree had become the place where the neighbours gathered. The zinc roofs heated up in the sunshine, making the mango tree the meeting place and providing much-needed shade. The tenants never planned these gatherings, but one tenant would sit under the Mango tree, and others would join in. However, there needed to be proper seating under the shady mango tree. Concrete blocks, old chairs with planks of wood and or drink crates, and anything that could provide seating was used. To Josephine, this was untidy, but no one else seemed to notice or care. In the summer months, the sweet smell of mango lingered in the air as the tenants bought *Black Mango*, *Number 11*, *Hairy* and other mangos to share. Josephine recalls the sense of goodwill that she felt as she observed the neighbours' kindness towards each other.

The mango tree was tall, and its branches were wide, casting long shadows in different directions as the sun moved through the sky throughout the day. The declaration, *"Mi si a mango,"* was a refrain that would bring much excitement. The tree's trunk was thick and gnarly, with darker bumps or knots of brown in some areas. These bumps served as good footholds for the children when they climbed up the tree to pick a mango that had just started to turn in colour from green to yellow. *A turn mango* is a mango that is not fully ripe. If the mango had a good colour between green and yellow, that too was celebrated.

Minor accidents sometimes happened under the tree, as knees and toes got skinned and scraped. Unlike next door, where there was a giant mango tree from which a boy fell one day and had to be taken to the hospital in an ambulance. He survived, but his injuries were severe. Despite the danger, no *turn mango* was ever left to ripen, as having so many people watching the tree for fruits meant that the fruits needed to spend more time on the tree. A major 'score or find' meant you had spotted a mango and secured it by climbing the tree or throwing stones or other handy implements to knock it from its stem.

"Mi si a mango, mi si a mango, it ready like Freddy, Freddy, it ready like Freddy" was the song the children sang when they spotted a turn mango. The 'lucky' persons who picked turn mangoes would peel and eat them with salt added to the slices. At those times, it was not unusual to hear someone say, *"Mi mouth a run water,"* as watching someone else eat a *turn mango* would cause the observer to experience increased spittle in their mouths, much like what happens when you watch someone suck on a lime. Josephine recalls being sick to her stomach, as she heard the adults speculating one day, *"De root a de mango tree gaan dung ina di pit toilet."* It was unsettling for Josephine to overhear such discussions, but interestingly, she noticed that everyone was still happy to eat the fruits of the mango tree.

The ground of the tenement yard was all dirt, hard as clay in the dry months and muddy in the rainy season. This situation made Josephine very squeamish as she was not fond of mud. In the dry season, depending on the mood someone woke up with, there would be aggressive sweeping after using a bucket of water to sprinkle the ground to keep the dust from rising as they swept. The smell of the damp earth was very comforting. In those days, brooms were sometimes unavailable due to cost. That, however, did not stop an inspired sweeper from doing the job, as a bunch of branches tied together could do. Josephine thought when she saw this happening that the sweeper was a real *show-off*, making their broom.

There was no roster; it happened naturally. Whoever was in the mood swept. If someone was happy, then that person would sweep. If they were sad, they would sweep. Sweeping had magical powers as moods were better when the tenants swept the yard, or each tenant swept just outside their front door. Some people had a greater sense of pride in their surroundings, so much so that they would plant a mint bush, a pepper tree or a croton at the corner of their unit. Josephine remembers not liking the taste of mint tea but liking the smell of the mint bush when she crushed it between her fingers. Scary to her was the notion that if you smelled the mint in the dark of night, it meant that a ghost was nearby.

Over time, one or more tenants had planted various plants haphazardly. If a tenant went somewhere and got a *slip* of a plant or bush they admired, they would simply dig a hole and plant it. So at the entrance and along the fences were *Aloe Vera* plants, called *Single Bible*, *Crotons* in various colours, *Purple Hearts*, *Cana* Lillies and various bushes that survived independently. Any hardy enough plant to survive on its own was used, as once planted, it was hardly ever tended to again. To this end, Josephine planted a pumpkin seed one day, and soon, to her delight, a vine was running everywhere!

The yard was alive, with activity in the mornings as people got ready for work and in the evenings when they returned and started to prepare their meals. During the days, there was usually a lull, which brought calm and a sense of peace to the compound. Dogs slept under trees or the cellars. Children went to school, and adults who worked away from the yard went to work; each period of the day comforted Josephine as it was familiar and welcoming. During the school holidays, she loved the lazy slowness of the middays, as the children would play in the mornings or attend a makeshift summer school nearby, which would end by midday. They would come home for lunch, usually porridge; they ate under the shady mango tree while waiting for the sun to 'cool off.'

Josephine preferred evenings best during school time, as stories that started in the mornings would continue during the evenings, and she would hear how a story ended. A lot of storytelling happened at this time, usually by the older children. Ghost stories, eyewitness stories of strange happenings, recounting the details of quarrels, etc. There were always things to talk about during that time. Josephine always had her own story to tell; "*Yu* know *sey,* last night *mi* hear a rolling calf when mi di go *fi* get *wata*", said Josephine.

"*Yu neva* hear *nuting!*" said Jeanie, Juwan's younger sister.

"Yes, ask Mama. She go call *Misa* Francis, *an im sey mi 'ed raise big,*" *dramatised Josephine with her hands.*

"*Mi see* de black heart man last night, an '*im yey dem* red," said *Juwan* pointing to her rolling eyes for emphasis.

"We-eeey?" asked Carla, looking around hysterically.

"*Ina de* back *yaad,* and '*im* step *ova de* fence when '*im si mi,*" said Juwan mimicking how he went over the fence.

"Yu know *sey,* if *yu* put *yu* big toe pon *mi* big toe while *mi* a eat *sumting,* it can go *ina* your belly *tu?"* asked Carla. *"Everybody know dat,"* everyone said, matter of fact.

The stories were many as the children spent much time together.

In the mornings, the adults would share their dreams. Josephine would be listening keenly as she loved the phrase, "Last night, *mi did dream sey."* The adults would then discuss and share what they thought their dreams meant. These were very much like Josephine's imaginings, and she found them enjoyable to listen to. The interpretations offered for the dreams were equally exciting but a bit scary for her. These usually had a sense of dread and foreboding that Josephine did not like.

It seemed to Josephine that the adults used dreams to foretell the future, so dreaming about a dead loved one could mean an impending death. Deaths supposedly came in threes, so after one death, they expected two more. Baby deaths were especially scary for Josephine as she heard someone say one day that a baby ghost did not know what they were doing, so they could hurt you.

In the evenings, a similar 'buzz' of greetings was exchanged, and relevant gossip and news items were shared among the tenants. The children, too, would commence their activities such as playing, washing uniforms, cleaning shoes, doing homework, etc. If a shared dream and its interpretation were ever remotely realised, then the buzz in the evening would reach a high level.

Josephine recalls the buzz one evening in the yard when a man in a common law relationship seemed to have died on his job as a linesman at the **Jamaica Public Service Company.** He had been electrocuted. According to the adults, he was abusive to his partner, and she had asked God that very morning to rescue her from her situation. Immediately hearing that, Josephine thought, *Jezam,* weezam, *God strike him dead!*

The excitement was twofold. The man died after his partner prayed. Secondly, his death puzzled Josephine as some unknown person handed him a handkerchief containing 'some nasty sup'um' according to the adults. Josephine never understood what was in the kerchief and how it caused him to die, but the adults all seemed to understand what it was. He had looked inside the folded kerchief and, after that, climbed up the 'light pole' he was supposed to work on without turning off the power and was electrocuted.

Try as she might, Josephine's imagination could not figure out what was in the handkerchief and why it was important. She felt sorry that the man had died and was not sure who she should be afraid of, the common law partner, God or whatever was in the kerchief. Based on what the adults said, Josephine knew something supernatural had happened. This sudden death was just one of the never-ending occurrences in the yaad.

There was usually lots of loud laughter, singing, talking, preaching, and music. Occasionally, a resident who felt the need to '**Rock Steady**' loudly would set up an extensive sound system. It was not unusual to hear *'tracing'* (quarrelling) among the women especially. The objective was to speak your mind on a topic loudly over your opponent in as colourful a language as possible. Jamaican expletives mostly surround body parts and fabric. Speaking one's mind was a good thing. It meant that you were not a hypocrite; your behaviour was due to your birth sign, and so, *is jus so yu stay.* "*Mi born June or January yu nuh, mi a go chat mi mine.*" A *tracer would* say. This way of settling differences allows you to act without accountability and with wanton disregard for anyone else's feelings. This code of conduct meant your body parts or your mother's parts were fair game; the more offensive, the better. Such situations would result in a time of *'malice'* where people did not speak directly to each other for a while. The usual peacemakers in the yaad would sometimes have to intervene.

The women shared their lives and their stories with each other. They commiserated with each other when their partners did not live up to their expectations. There was transparency among them and genuine friendships. Even though most worked to feed their families, they were always present. They held the families together while suffering from being overworked, underpaid and under-appreciated by their partners and sometimes being cheated on and physically abused, too. It seemed that talking with each other gave them the relief they needed to continue their life's journey.

The men operated on the far fringes of Josephine's consciousness. They were there but mainly as shadows in a dim room. Occasionally, a man would step into the light, and she would get a look at him. The men mostly drank to excess, occasionally visiting as they had more than one family or had no opinion on topics other than sports, as they sat under the mango tree listening to a horse race on the radio or writing on racing forms that bore the names of horses and schedules of races. Sometimes, they could be seen rolling a *spliff* to smoke. The lone exception was Mr Francis, who was always present, consistently doing activities with his family and providing for them. He was an excellent example to his neighbours; his presence was positive and uplifting to those around him.

The *tenement yaad* was but one yard among other properties. There were neighbours at various stages of social transitioning. Some owned their property but wanted to migrate uptown to newer communities like **Havendale, Hughenden, Patrick City, Pembroke Hall,** etc. Some were too invested in their property, so they could not leave, like the family that owned cows and sold the milk and the families that still lived there and relied on renting quarters to supplement their income.

The yard was a living, breathing space that Josephine enjoyed being a part of; it was a school for life. The children were fed and clothed, nothing fancy, enough to keep alive their childlike qualities and sustain hopes and dreams. *The Tenement Yaad* itself was safe and nurturing for Josephine. It operated as a village, and children were raised by all the adults in the village. It felt accepting, and she knew she belonged there instead of being with either side of her parents' families.

Jamaica back then was operated with more civility. People seemed more caring, and life's pace was slower. Josephine loved her life in the yaad; everything she needed was there. *Mango Tree, me an yu a best fren don't it?* She whispered. Josephine was happy that she could always imagine away all her cares with the Mango tree, her best friend, and when she got bored, there was always something to watch and wonder about in the yaad. *Dis ya yaad ya, fulla excitement*, thought Josephine, as she watched her mother walk into the tenement yaad through the faded green gate, her hands filled with packages. A surge of joy filled her contented heart. "Mama, come! Mama, come!" She shouted to Carla inside the house and ran excitedly towards the green gate to meet her. She was home at last.

Dedicated to Josephines' Papa and Mama who made home safe and happy.

Glossary

Cilla Black - Was a popular British star in the 1960s and later a famous TV presenter in the 1980s.

John Davison - American actor, singer and game show host.

Kerchief - Handkerchief

Rock Steady - is an early form of reggae music originating in Jamaica in the 1960s, characterised by a slow tempo.

Tom Jones - Multi-award winning Welsh singer who became popular in the 1960s and is still enjoying world wide acclaim.

Slip - A Cutting from a mature plant made to replant elsewhere.

Spittle - Saliva

Spliff - Dried Marijuana/Ganja leaves rolled into smoking paper for smoking.

Mutts - A word used to describe animals [people] of mixed breeding.

MAMA FOWL LAY!

Josephine, and her older sister Carla lived together in *The Tenement Yaad* in Kingston, Jamaica, in the mid-1960s. The age difference between the girls posed a challenge. Josephine was younger, and so they were not playmates. Carla had a girlfriend named Joan, who was her age, with whom she played most of the time. Carla enjoyed teasing Josephine by pulling her hair or pinching her when no adults were around to see her. Carla also laughed uncontrollably when she thought something was funny. Teasing her sister and laughing went together. Carla tormented her little sister while Joan watched and laughed.

Josephine's way to retaliate was to tattle and whine. She became known among the adults as 'miserable' as she constantly complained.

In truth, Josephine felt trapped, unable to fight her older and bigger sister even though she tried. She was particularly resentful of Carla's friendship with Joan, (pronounced 'Juwan') in the Jamaican dialect, because it meant Carla always had an audience to play up to. Josephine liked Juwan but was resentful of Carla's friendship with her as they tormented her together. Together with Carla, she made Josephine's life unbearable. They would wreck her make-believe houses, erase her road lanes in the dirt, pull on her crazy, curly hair and even pinch her and then run away laughing. Josephine felt helpless, angry and frustrated. If she tried to complain to the adults around, they would say, "Neva mine, gwaan go play." They did not give the complaints too much attention. Also, the older girls would hide and tease Josephine to frustration.

Juwan was considered to be fat, a recognition she relished. *"Lawd you maaga eeh?"* She would say to Carla and Josephine. This expression was how Jamaicans described skinny people. They believed that being fat meant you were healthy and prosperous. *Juwan* certainly had high self-esteem, despite being born with a deformed left hand, having only a thumb and a little finger. Her disability, however, did not cause *Juwan* any setbacks. She did everything well. *"Mi* can wash and clean *betta dan unnu."* She would say to the other children as if to prove her point. *Juwan* had a cheerful face and short plaited hair, sometimes worn in two puffs. She was good-tempered and obedient to her mother, Miss Beryl. She is another story to tell.

Juwan's mother, Miss Beryl, was an exceptionally distinctive figure to Josephine. She was very businesslike and owned and operated a rum bar. As a business owner, she was confident and seemed to be quite 'knowledgeable' about matters such as money, men and disciplining children. Miss Beryl was not very tall, but that is where her inadequacies ended. Weighing about two hundred and ten pounds, she was purposefully oversized, fulfilling the local maxim – *the bigger, the better and the more prosperous.*

Josephine thought it unusual that Miss Beryl wore her hair in a low afro, as except for 'Christians' most women in Miss Beryl's position, being a rum bar owner, would hot comb their hair to straighten it and then do 'drop curls.' Josephine thought that the low haircut added to Miss Beryl's air of confidence and power. Black in complexion until her skin shone, she had a round, expressive face that was quick to laugh but also quick to show her displeasure. She had a swift temper, sharp tongue and reputation as a *'good beater.'* Woe be unto anyone caught in one of her beatings!

In her usual business-like manner, Miss Beryl bought a laying hen and raised it with great fanfare, anticipating the day it would start producing eggs. Soon, everyone knew of her foray into the poultry business. When she deemed the fowl mature enough by inserting her finger daily into the reproductive orifice of the bird, she determined that her investment would produce an egg any day soon.

As it happened, she was correct. With only the three playmates around one afternoon, Miss Beryl's fowl started to squawk, announcing having laid an egg. The children were very excited, *Juwan* especially had an added sense of pride because her mother owned the fowl. With unthinking childishness, she fetched the egg from the chicken coop and danced about, singing, "*Mama fowl lay, Mama fowl lay...*" What a joyous bunch they were that day, *Juwan*, Carla and Carla's little sister Josephine as they danced and sang, '*Mama fowl lay, Mama fowl lay.*' It was genuine joy and wonder at this marvel of nature.

This larger-than-life moment, which should have been enriching and encouraging, not to mention nourishing to whoever would have the good fortune to taste the egg, took a sad turn. As the children all celebrated, *Juwan*, whether because of her deformed hand or out of careless exuberance, had an accident that would haunt her for a long time.

She dropped the egg. Sploooatt! It broke.

The silence that followed after such jubilation was deafening. As *Juwan* looked at the splintered shell on the ground, Josephine saw that her face had changed from joy to shock to terror. The scene changed so quickly, but Josephine was able to record it in her mind as *Juwan's* facial muscles changed from flexibly laughing to disbelief, which made her seem rigid and unsure of what had just happened. *Juwan's* body became tense as she slowly appeared to understand the implications of what she had done. She would surely get a beating! Even Carla was looking at her with sorrow. This accident was no laughing matter.

Recovering quickly, Carla said, "*Nu worry, Juwan, mek we preten we don't know nuttin.*"

Juwan, recovering more slowly, still looking doubtful, sighed a sigh of relief.

"Yu sure?" Juwan asked Carla.

Carla turned to Josephine and said, *"If you tell, Juwan a go get a beating."* Josephine agreed not to '*tell,*' and *Juwan* agreed to the plan. The two sisters decided that to save *Juwan* from a bad beating from Miss Beryl, they would pretend that nothing had happened, and at that moment when they were all in agreement, Josephine felt good. The bigger girls had included her in their secret. Josephine had every intention of not telling about the egg.

That evening, Miss Beryl came home, looked into the coop and felt the fowl's nether region for an egg. She was surprised that the fowl seemed to have laid, but the egg was not in the coop. Miss Beryl concluded that the hen must have laid her egg underneath one of the houses, and she commissioned the children to search the cellars in daylight. The search went on for days, and no one found the egg. Miss Beryl was puzzled but soon seemed to forget about the egg.

In the meantime, life returned to normal, and Carla and her side-kick *Juwan* resumed their torment of Josephine. Now, however, little Josephine realised that she could get Carla to stop teasing her because of the secret that all three children shared. She said, *"Juwan, tell yu friend to leave mi alone, or I will tell."* Juwan would plead with her friend Carla, to desist from teasing Josephine. Using her hands by clasping them together as if in prayer or her eyes by opening them as wide as she could, or mutely mouthing *"please, Carla"*. Juwan would show her fear of getting a beating from her mother.

As time went on, *Juwan's* fears grew. Josephine's power swelled, and Carla's enjoyment and fits of giggles over the situation grew to hysterical proportions. There were several occasions in which Carla, while in the company of Miss Beryl, was reduced to tears due to her inability to control her laughter at *Juwan's* facial contortions, dramatic eye movements and muted appeals.

There would be gathered in the *yaad*, under the mango tree, a company of adults and children; Carla would pull on Josephine's ponytail, Josephine would let out a high whine, then turn to *Juwan* and say, "*Yu betta talk to yu frien, yu nuh.*" Carla would collapse into a heap of giggles, hiccups and tears, unable to contain her glee. Poor *Juwan* would appeal to Carla to stop while wringing her hands in distress. The cycle of taunts→ distress→ blackmail→ laughter→ appeal, and distress went on for weeks; each time, it was getting harder and harder for Carla to keep herself from laughing. The truth is that Josephine started to feel some remorse at becoming the tormentor herself as she empathised deeply with *Juwan's* distress but found it was the only way to stop her sister from persecuting her.

Josephine became desperate to stop her. Her threats to *Juwan* became obvious and loud. 'Sey *fey, mi tell*,' appealing to *Juwan* to reason with Carla to stop teasing her. *Juwan* did try and became desperate when Josephine started saying, "*Juwan, tell yu friend, fi leave me alone, or I will tell Miss Beryl wha happen to the egg.*"

Juwan would plead with her friend; "*Carla, leave ar alone, nuh.*" Carla would stop for a while, but the next day, the teasing would start again.

One day, while a gathering was under the mango tree, Mama proudly said, "*You know Sey Pertylou laid a double yoke egg yesterday?*" Mama had given her chicken a name. This announcement started a discussion about chickens.

"You know sey, mi chicken lay every day?" Said Miss Evadney, another tenant.

"*My chicken lay some big eggs,*" said Miss Hilda, yet another tenant.

"*Fi mi chicken a get ole, she* slowing down on the laying," said Miss Willy's girlfriend.

Josephine knew what happened to the chickens when they got too old to lay eggs. She was not happy with Miss Willy's girlfriend's grave tone because the next step would be to have that chicken for Sunday dinner at the soonest convenience. The talk of chickens made *Juwan* visibly sweat!

Carla was busy laughing as if without reason; "*A wat wrong wid da pickney ya?*"

Miss Willy's girlfriend asked.

"*A so Carla stay,*" said Mama. "*She no have nuting fi worry ar.*"

Nevertheless, the tormenting cycle continued every day. As expected, each participant's resolve started to wear thin. On a hot afternoon, under the shady mango tree, thankfully before an audience, Carla tugged, Josephine whined, and Juwan implored with her eyes. Carla's tug on Josephine's ponytail was followed by her uncontrollable giggling. A high-pitched, "Carla, stop it!, *Juwan* talk to yu fren," erupted from Josephine. Then, streaming tears and cackling laughter bubbled out of Carla. A desperate *Juwan* pleaded in a whisper, "Carla, leave ar alone, nuh?"

As old-time Jamaicans would say, it was the 'straw that broke the camel's back', and Josephine said determinedly, "Miss Beryl..."

Miss Beryl answered, "What, Josephine?"

Looking at fretting *Juwan*, Josephine answered, "Nuttin."

Juwan looked pleadingly at Carla. Carla, laughing still, pulled on Josephine's hair <u>again.</u>

"Miss Beryl, Yu know sey...." continued Josephine, stopping short each time and not 'telling.' By then, Miss Beryl and the other adults were curious about what Josephine had to say. They had started to see the dynamics among the girls and realised that Josephine had a story to tell. Carla tugged her hair again, but now, with all eyes focused on her, Josephine blurted out, "*Juwan brok yu egg, Miss Beryl.*"

Juwan's look of utter dread was a '**Kodak** moment' if ever there was one. Today, that image would trend as a meme. With her face contorted with anxiety and her palms sweating, she kept moving her palms down her skirt almost in anticipation, preparing them for Miss Beryl's 'licks.' *Juwan* quickly explained what had happened all those weeks ago. "*Mama mi sarry, it was a accident, nu beat mi,*" pleaded *Juwan.*

The other tenants thought the whole thing was amusing. They marvelled that the girls thought that Josephine could keep a secret, and they laughed heartily. Miss Beryl's anger had since abated, and being in the company of other adults who were laughing at the whole situation, forced her to do likewise. "*My God! Unnu know how long mi a wonder wat happen to the egg?*" Said Miss Beryl.

Everyone had such a good laugh that *Juwan* was spared the long-anticipated beating. Josephine genuinely shared her relief at being spared and no longer having the axe of the secret hanging above her head. The group went on to other escapades, but Carla could always be reduced to a blubbering pile of laughter at the very hint of the tune, *"Mama fowl lay, Mama fowl lay."*

Dedicated to Josephine's sister, Carla, whom she loves and greatly admires.

J

Glossary

Kodak moment - A leading photography brand (Kodak) that became a popular term for a good picture opportunity.

Sey fey - A dare or a bet

MISS BERYL 'THE BEATER'

Miss Beryl was a larger-than-life personality that commanded attention in the tenement yard. She was the eldest child of her mother, who had married afterwards and had other children. She was like a friend to her mother, Miss Jenny, a sweet-spirited woman whom Josephine was quite fond of.

Miss Beryl was in her mid-thirties, 5 ft 2 inches tall, weighing about 210 pounds; she was Negro and dark in complexion; she had a brother, Lloydy, who was called 'Black & Shine'. Lloydy was born into the family, while Miss Jenny's husband was at war in England during the

Second World War. It was an open secret, but her husband seemed to have accepted the situation when he returned home.

Miss Beryl's skin was a bit lighter than Lloydy's and she missed the description of being 'black and shine.'

She mainly wore skirts that seemed to emphasise her posterior. She was also well endowed with a buxom bosom, so her blouses did little to hide her full breasts. She had a round face that usually shone with sweat from the effort of riding her bicycle, then a manly activity, or the exertion she expended on anything she was doing. She never did anything in half measures.

Miss Beryl was very confident, so other adults quickly discussed life's situations with her. Her face would get animated quickly as she was passionate about most topics. Miss Beryl was a paradox, a cheerful person who also brought cheer to those around her as she was quick to see the humour in situations. However, Miss

Beryl was a moody woman. Sometimes, 'she blew hot'; other times, 'she blew cold'. Sometimes, she was sweet as a ripe Julie Mango and at other times, she was as sour as Seville Orange. How she treated you depended on the mood she was in, and so generally, people in the tenement *yaad* learned to take her as she came and not judge her too harshly because, you see, she was a very nice woman, as long as you didn't get on her wrong side. She had a serious temper when provoked and didn't have the patience for too much talking; she simply eliminated the source of her provocation by physically removing the disturbance.

Miss Beryl could be very violent. She would literally 'knock sense into you' if you were talking nonsense and 'lick the living daylight out of you' if you threatened her or her loved ones. She would volunteer to 'teach you a lesson' if you tested her patience. Her most distinctive talent was being a no-nonsense 'beater' of her children and boyfriends. At those times, out in the open and with witnesses, she would apply her licks to the offending party without anyone objecting to her behaviour. This violence was a source of much tension and fear in the yaad, so all who knew what would provoke her deliberately tried to hide infractions from Miss Beryl.

Miss Beryl was the most outgoing and 'worldly' of all the tenants in the yaad. Miss Beryl attended stage shows and, when she returned to the yaad, would regale the other tenants with her pick of which singers were the best. According to Miss Beryl, **Ken Boothe** was a good singer, **Toots and the Maytals** were great, and **The Wailers** had potential. She said it, and all the other tenants accepted it as truth.

Josephine recalls one morning, Miss Beryl giving the recap of a show she had attended the night before, where a little boy, **Junior Tucker**, had sung. She was very impressed by the child's talents but worried that "*him too young to open im 'pores so much.*" Josephine found herself worrying about **Junior Tucker's** 'pores'. It seems Miss Beryl was worried that the young man might hurt his vocal chords to be singing so well at such a young age.

It was also Miss Beryl who always knew what fashion, fabrics and colours were being worn for the festival and Independence celebrations. Josephine often wondered how she knew. Nevertheless, everyone usually followed her declarations, and those who could afford it would purchase the fabric and be decked out in their Independence outfits on August 6th each year.

Miss Beryl was a natural leader, and so was usually front and centre among the adults in the yard, who, on Easter Sunday mornings, would break an egg, separate the yolk from the 'white' albumen of the egg and then put the 'white' into a glass with water and leave it on the roof of the fowl coop. Everyone believed an image would form as the rising sun shone on the 'white' in the water. They then interpreted the formed image in the glass superstitiously. All the adults waited with bated breath and hoped to see a ship in their glass. A ship would mean that their future held the possibility of migration to a better land such as the USA, Canada or England. Josephine watched this process in fascination each year and remembers one young woman named Teresa, who eventually left for Canada. Mostly, Josephine saw formations that looked like clouds, no particular shape, but each year, the shapes brought new hope for the adults.

Josephine recalls feeling frightened and sorry for Miss Beryl's boyfriend one evening as dusk fell. His name was Mr Austin, and he was a mild-mannered man who always seemed to be waiting on Miss Beryl to speak so that he could do her bidding. Miss Beryl seemed proud to have Mr Austin as her boyfriend as he was a handsome, light-skinned man who was half her size. His size made it easy for her to overpower him and sit on top of him in a fight. On this night, he managed to escape her grasp and ran to

Josephine's house for shelter from Miss Beryl's beating. The commotion made Josephine frightened and afraid that someone would get hurt and the police would have to be called. However, even though he was not too seriously hurt, by the time Mama and Papa rescued him, he was already bleeding from a cut on his forehead where she had hit him with a wash pan made of aluminium. Mr Austin survived the beatings and went on to have a long relationship with Miss Beryl.

She was a single mother to two girls. Joan, ten years old, was one of her two daughters. The other daughter was Jeanie; she was eight years old and tall with long, gangly legs, a sly girl who could lie and cry on cue. Miss Beryl had a weakness for her younger daughter, which Josephine could not understand because she made Jeannie get away with so much that everyone in the yaad could see it was just another of her sly tricks.

Her older daughter Joan, whose name was

mispronounced by everyone as *Juwan* was rightfully afraid of Miss Beryl. Josephine was confused whenever Miss Beryl would so easily beat *Juwan* but bragged to anyone who cared to listen that she was proud of her daughter as she could do everything as 'gud' or better than other children. This boasting might have been because *Juwan* had the disadvantage of being born with a deformed left hand. *Juwan's* left hand resembled the claw of a crab. She had a thumb and one little finger. However, *Juwan* did everything as well as the rest of the children, and she even did more in terms of housework, washing etc., for fear of being beaten by Miss Beryl.

One would have thought she would naturally protect Joan because of her disability. In Miss Beryl's logic, she was the older child and was held responsible for her younger siblings' behaviour. To Josephine, this made Miss Beryl's feigned ignorance of Jeannie's behaviour a puzzle to be continuously solved because otherwise, Miss Beryl, it seemed, knew everything!

Having witnessed her beating *Juwan* on multiple occasions, Josephine's senses were usually alert to Miss Beryl's mood. She was not afraid of Miss Beryl for herself but was afraid for Miss Beryl's family's sake. The tension would increase in the yard, and Josephine would feel her heartbeats speed up when Miss Beryl came home. Miss Beryl's daughters would usually try to look busy at those times. The tension would stay heightened until everyone knew she was not about to find fault with anything. Then, Josephine would feel her breath go back to normal.

One day, Miss Beryl discovered someone had used her *Cutex* nail polish. She was furious; *"Which one of unno use mi* Cutex?" She demanded to know. Both girls said under the mango tree and with witnesses, *"A nuh me, Mama."* However, the evidence was on Jeannie's fingers as her attempts to wipe the polish from her nails were inadequate, and traces of the polish were still evident. To the amusement of the adults present and the anguish of the other children. With tears running down her face, Jeanne denied it was her; *"A nuh me mama."* Miss Beryl proceeded to beat *Juwan; "You a the older one and shoulda able fi sey a who du it."* She said as she hit *Juwan.*

Josephine still recalls the trauma of watching Miss Beryl beat *Juwan.* Feeling afraid for *Juwan,* upset, and helpless, Josephine felt like there was a roaring sound in her head as Miss Beryl repeatedly hit *Juwan* with her fists or open hands and anything else she could find. Josephine felt like hiding her face as it got hot, and her heartbeat raced quickly. Miss Beryl's temper grew as she beat *Juwan,* making her seem even angrier. *Juwan* was like a trapped animal, not even allowed to run as her mother said, *"If you run, I kill yu!"*

Juwan cried and repeatedly said, *"Mi sarry Mama, mi sarry Mama,"* as her mother was hitting her. Eventually, after tiring herself out, Miss Beryl stopped beating her, complained to the transfixed audience that Juwan caused her to get tired, and walked off in a huff.

Psychologists today would classify Miss Beryl as being a physical and emotional abuser of *Juwan*. They would perhaps explain her ill-treatment by saying she was expressing her hurt and disappointment at having a child who was physically disabled. To Josephine and others who lived in the *yaad*, Miss Beryl was just plain cruel to *Juwan* and nobody had the nerve to challenge her about it.

Also living in the yard was an Indian man and his girlfriend and baby. They shared part of a two-room structure with a locked door between the rooms. The locked door led to Miss Beryl's room. They seemed very quiet and did not interact much with the other tenants; they did not get a chance to stay long as an incident forced them to leave. This one incident caused Josephine more dismay, as well as puzzlement, than any other. The mystery of the Indian man, his girlfriend, and Miss Beryl remained unsolved in Josephine's mind for a long time.

One morning around 8 o'clock, hearing a commotion, Josephine came out as raised voices usually meant a 'tracing match' was starting or neighbours were on the brink of a fight.

"*Unnu, outta orda, unnu just come ya, and unnu go du dis.*" Said Miss Beryl.

"*Wi nuh know what yu talking bout.*" said the Indian man.

"*"Yeh, we nuh know wey yu a talk bout.*" said His girlfriend, with much bravado.

As other tenants gathered around, the couple and Miss Berly exchanged further words as the argument heated up.

"*Unnu a big people, unnu shoud'en du dat,*" said Miss Beryl. "*Lef dat to de pickney dem man. If a pickney di du dat, it wouda bad but nuh so bad.*"

The other tenants, looking on, were starting to sense that the couple did not realise that they were 'playing with fire' by answering back to Miss Beryl. They all knew to ignite Miss Beryl was to create an out-of-control blaze. "Alright, Beryl, never mind, *mi understan* why yu upset," said Mama, as she realised that the couple thought they could match Miss Beryl word for word without severe consequences.

"Yes, Beryl, it is okay," said Miss Evadney, another tenant.

As if to bolster their claim of innocence, the girlfriend shouted at Beryl;

"*We neva duh nu-tin, a lie yu a* tell." said the girlfriend. At this statement, Miss Beryl stepped back, momentarily seeming off-balanced; she took a sharp breath as if someone had slapped her.

"*A wey yu sey to me, gal?*" she retorted. "*Wey yu sey?*" "*Mi- a -tell -lie?*" *Yu know who yu a fool wid gal?*"

As new tenants, the couple did not know Miss Beryl was not to be trifled with. They thought that they could defend themselves verbally. That, however, was a mistake. The Indian man realised that Miss Beryl had assumed a fighting stance. He noticed the growing anger within Miss Beryl as her cheeks were puffed out, and her breathing had become short as she struggled to control her emotions. He placed his girlfriend, who was resisting him, inside their door. Still trying not to seem intimidated, after all, he was a man, and Miss Beryl was a woman. He now positioned himself in his doorway, but the door was halfway closed. As he was about to say something else, suddenly, Miss Beryl lunged at him.

"Come yah!" she said, trying to grab him.

Luckily, he was swift, evaded her reach, and quickly closed his door with a slam. Beryl shouted and pounded on the door, demanding they come out as she would deal with them. Using expletives and physical force against the door, she continued until she was sweaty and spent before she started to calm down. By this time, she was sweating so much that she walked away to get a towel to wipe her face.

Josephine imagined the couple inside, cowering in a corner as Miss Beryl beat down their door. Hearing the commotion, Mr Francis appeared and asked, "What is happening out here? Why is Beryl causing all this commotion?"

"Missa Francis, Beryl mad as hell as she ketch dem a peep pon ar an Mr Austin de odda night tru the keyhole," said Evadney, the neighbour.

"Me say, me jus in time fi see Beryl lick afta de man an a threaten fi beat them to penny crease," she said excitedly. *"A gud ting 'im quick cause Beryl wouda poun 'im."* She added for effect.

All gathered would have been able to imagine the beating the man would have received had he been caught. At that very moment, Miss Beryl reappeared, towel in hand, and told Mr

Francis what had caused her temper to rise. Visibly trying to calm her temper by wiping her face, in her unabashed worldly way, she explained, *"Mi an Austin did in deh a sucu- rucu and dem have di nerve fi a peep pon wi.' Mi sey, dem outta orda an deserve a beating."* Arms akimbo and her stance set for war, she showed her indignation. *"Wat kinda ting dat?"* *"Yu wrong mi, Mr Francis?"* she asked. Mr Francis looked a little sheepish and chuckled self-consciously. "No, Beryl, I understand why you are upset." He answered her, looking flushed in the face.

It took Josephine a long time to decipher what Miss Beryl was upset about. *"A whe you a say to me?"* Inquired another neighbour who had just joined the group, inching closer to Miss Beryl to get the full story. Miss Beryl rehashed the whole story with much anger, intermittently wiping her forehead with her towel as she went on.

That night, the couple left under the 'cloak of darkness' after staying locked in their room for the rest of the day. The next morning, Papa awoke and asked Mama what had happened. "*Tin Tin, last night mi see* the young couple *wey* just move in leaving and *dem neva say nuting tu mi.* Me think *it strange cause* dem was always very respectful to me."

Mama explained to him what had transpired the day before. Others heard the exchange as they stood around the communal standpipe while Papa brushed his teeth. According to him, very late that night, '*when dog fraid*', they left and went to safety. Papa had seen them leaving very late the night before as he was coming home after a late night of drinking.

"*Lawd hav* mercy, now, we understand why *dem* disappear," said another tenant who did not know what had happened, "We *dun* know sey Beryl she *nuh* joke!" Everybody nodded in agreement at this remark, muttering," Umm, Ummm, Umm, as if singing a round. Later in the day, Miss Beryl's anger abated to the point where her neighbours could jokingly ask her what '*Sucu Rucu*' meant while they all laughed, including Miss Beryl. Meanwhile, Josephine was glad things calmed down but was still annoyed that the adults were not explaining things so she could understand.

The couple had their belongings brought to them rather than return to the tenement *yaad* for them. That couple and the baby were never seen again. Even though it seems the man was able to close his door quickly and was not harmed, Josephine felt unsettled about the whole issue. Josephine was mainly upset because the man was referred to repeatedly as a 'two-fi one', which Josephine knew was a derogatory way of describing an East Indian person. Josephine wondered if everybody disliked him because of his ethnicity. She concluded that it could not have been the case as the neighbours regarded her Mama well, and she was East Indian, too.

To Josephine's innocent mind, the camaraderie and easy interaction between neighbours of different ethnic groups were confounding as they could easily change into calling each other unkind names. When a negro boy was 'held up' at knifepoint by an Indian boy, his mother was obviously worried about the safety of her son. However, as soon as she had established that he was unharmed, her following statement bewildered Josephine. *"It bad enough dat dem hole him up, but it worsa 'cause it's a **&%$**ing two-fi one."* Josephine wondered, *'Why the lady cursing? Me tink say she was glad har son alrite.'* So often, when adults spoke, the more profound sociological implications eluded Josephine for many years.

The tenement *yaad* was a microcosm of the larger society. Rich with culture, ripe with nuances and riddled with contradictions, Josephine loved it all. She enjoyed knowing each person and recalls that most people lived their 'better side' most of the time.

As an adult, Josephine recalls them all fondly, including Miss Beryl.

Glossary

Cutex - A popular brand nail polish

Junior Tucker - Leslie Tucker, known professionally as Junior Tucker, is a Jamaican reggae singer, who started his career as a child.

Ken Boothe - Kenneth George Boothe OD is an internationally acclaimed Jamaican vocalist known for his distinctive voice.

Sucu rucu - having sex

Toots and the Maytals - Toots and the Maytals, are an internationally renown Jamaican musical group, which polularised ska and rocksteady.

THE CRIPPLED PUPPY

Josephine viewed the world through the lens of a vast playground. Play was necessary, and formal activities were less readily available, such as music lessons or swimming, but she had friends, a yard to play their games and her best friend, the mango tree.

The mango tree was her haven, her imaginarium where she felt such a sense of peace under its shade in the lull of a day when hardly anyone else was around. She would sit and use a stick, idly draw figures in the dirt, and enjoy a good time imagining. At those times, Josephine imagined herself to be like *Huckleberry Finn* or *Pollyanna*, children in stories she had heard about. They, too, enjoyed being outside in the sunshine, running barefoot and free to idle the day away.

Josephine felt that the mango tree, like her, heard all that the adults said when they gathered under its branches. "*Wat Mr Francis mean when 'im sey dem heng up Jesus pan a cross?*" "*How 'ole are you?*" "*You know wey the people in dat room gaan?*" Josephine would ask the tree question after question and supply the answers from her imagination.

She thought she and the mango tree had a good relationship as she spent time alone under its shade. She enjoyed the rough feel of its trunk and thought its branches and leaves were beautiful as they waved and seemed to dance and shimmer in the breeze and sunlight. Josephine heard gentle whispering sounds as the light wind moved the leaves and imagined the hand of God making the branches of trees.

God hand dem must be big, big, big, to create de whole world, she thought.

Josephine was mostly obedient. She attended school, church, and Sunday School and sometimes visited her mother's relatives on school holidays. Even though Josephine's perspective was that of a carefree little girl, this did not mean she was unaware of the family's situation.

Josephine was intuitive and took initiative even as a young child. She sensed her and her sister's place in their extended families early on. Knowing they were considered poor relations, Josephine knew who favoured them and who did not. She learned to survive among other people and children who lived in the same yard with her and her family. Josephine was even called 'Madda Peppa' because some adults thought she was too opinionated for her age.

She lived with her mother, father, and elder sister Carla, among other families in similar circumstances as her family, in a big tenement yaad.

Josephine's family did not have many material possessions. They were considered poor. Her understanding of being poor was that there was not always enough to eat. Josephine, however, loved her family and did not see their lack. She enjoyed having hot Milo when they had it or just hot condensed milk when **Milo** was unavailable. Sometimes, their hot beverage was mint tea. There were times when the family had crackers bought by the dozen, with **Anchor Butter** (which they called 'Best Butter'), to spread on the crackers, or when they had a whole pack of **Excelsior Crackers** but no butter. Like most children, Josephine and Carla much preferred snacks to meals and so to them each day was different but good.

Like most children, Josephine and Carla much preferred snacks to meals. So they had this when dinner was unavailable, on 'Ben Johnson Day'. This referred to Thursday, the day before payday, which is Friday. In Jamaican folklore, Ben Johnson was an overseer who worked on a plantation. Everyone had spent all their meagre wages by Thursday, and *Mr Ben Johnson* could be relied upon to bring the weekly wage on Thursday nights. Most Thursdays, only canned food was left in the cupboard, and there was only money to buy meat on Fridays. For Josephine, a can of corned beef and bread was something she relished; it was called a **Bully Beef** sandwich. She counted it as a perfect day. After all, Josephine and Carla did not care for rice and liver, oxtail, curried goat, or pig trotters. Instead, they were happy getting bun and cheese sandwiches, **Cheese Krunches**, biscuits, and other snacks.

Josephine enjoyed the companionship of other children who lived in her yard. As children in the *yaad*, none of them had formal play activities.

The children who lived in the same yard with Josephine played mostly *Hopscotch, Football*

(Soccer), Marbles, Jacks, and ball games together, and the boys had slingshots. Among the children, lively competitions developed as they improved their physical skills and coordination by playing outdoor games.

Josephine was not good at the games, but she played anyway. Hopscotch taught jumping and balancing as the children drew squares in the dirt in the shape of a cross with a smaller cross on top of it. When you jumped, all the squares had to be big enough to land in. Four squares, followed by three squares across at the top of those squares, were followed by one square on top, then three squares at the very top. The player threw a marker, usually made from something flat and round with a bit of weight, like a stone, to a specific square, and then they had to jump over the marker to land on the correct square.

Marbles also tested the coordination and skill of hitting a target by eyeing it and flicking the marble with your thumb. The game of Jacks taught balance and coordination, too. To Josephine, it was wonderful to watch a girl who could coordinate all the elements of the *Jacks*, which were ten or twelve small, light, plastic, multi-spiked objects. On top of her hand, she balanced all the jacks. She deftly threw the small plastic ball up in the air while flicking her hand over to have the *Jacks* land in her palm, catching the ball at the same time. As much as Josephine tried, she was just not very good at this.

All the games taught numbers and cooperation as the children kept scores. When disagreements arose, they were usually resolved cordially by the children.

Those were happy days for Josephine. She learned skills, decision-making, and independence. Life was simple. The children were free to run, play, and decide what to do.

In Josephine's yard, there were always dogs. They had specific owners, but most people liked them and treated them well, and the children enjoyed having the animals around. If a dog had puppies, the children would enjoy them until their cuteness waned.

One day, one of the dogs from the *yaad* had puppies, and Josephine chose a puppy from the litter and called it her own. No one objected. As far as Josephine remembers, the puppy was no longer still sucking milk from its mother.

It had shaggy hair and was the colour of wheat mixed in with brown and black. The puppy was a mongrel, not a fact that Josephine was aware of, but one that would not have mattered to her anyway. Pedigree animals were not 'in fashion' where Josephine lived at the time. Instead, Josephine remembers that the standard of beauty for dogs when she was growing up was whether they were shaggy or not. This puppy was shaggy, so to Josephine, he was beautiful. She spent many happy hours playing with the puppy before and after school.

One day, Josephine sprung up from bed, unable to contain her anticipation and ran to play with her puppy. On this day, however, her excitement soon faltered, as her little playmate did not greet her with the usual spirited yelping, jumping and licking. Instead, her beloved pet just lay in one position and whimpered in pain. Even to a small child of six years, it was evident that something was wrong. Cradling her pet, Josephine tried to comfort the puppy as best she could. These were not days of pet's rights. No one could afford to call a Vet. These were times when pets lived outside, ate table scraps, and did not require much maintenance and upkeep. Such were social conditions that the focus was on feeding the human family and providing for that unit's basic needs. Josephine, therefore, had no one to run to for help with her pet. After close inspection, she became angry that someone had hurt the puppy by possibly stepping on it, and she quickly knew what she had to do. She would take care of her puppy by herself.

Josephine had gone to Sunday school, and her teacher taught her that Jesus loves little children and animals and would answer prayers if asked. Josephine decided to ask Jesus to help her to look after her puppy and to make it walk again. Starting that first day, Josephine customarily shared her breakfast of crackers, tea, porridge, bread, and egg with her pet. She would clean it and place it in the shade of the mango tree before she went to school. Every evening, she would run home from school to feed the puppy, give it water and place it in an area of her yard where it would be safe and dry.

Josephine also did one other thing twice daily: pray that her puppy would walk again. If Josephine went to the toilet, she would clasp her hands, close her eyes and ask Jesus to make her puppy walk again. When she took her shower, she would find time, amidst soaping up and rinsing off, to clasp her hands, close her eyes and ask Jesus to make her puppy walk again. Josephine always remembered to pray.

Josephine and her pet developed a morning feeding and cleaning schedule they both looked forward to and enjoyed. The puppy could no longer run to greet Josephine, but his eyes would light up with excitement every morning that Josephine came to get it before she went to school. As she fed and cleaned him, he would lick her face as if to contribute to their shared time. Josephine placed her pet lovingly in a safe spot each day, telling him she would return later. Each evening, he would be there waiting expectantly for her return.

The days turned into weeks, and the weeks into months. The puppy became strong enough to pull itself around the yard despite his legs not working. This disability didn't deter Josephine from praying and looking after her puppy. Does it sound like Josephine and the crippled puppy were the only two creatures around? It would appear so since Josephine was so keen to see the puppy become well again that she almost forgot that she had other playmates and neighbours. The other children and adults living together yet separately in their houses in the big Tenement Yaad seemed to fade into the background, and her puppy took 'centre stage'.

All the tenants gave their opinions about Josephine's caring for a useless animal, including the neighbours across the fence with a red-coat plum tree in their yard.

They owned their property, which immediately elevated their status compared to the tenants in Josephine's yaad. Mr. and Mrs. Holness and their daughter, Miss Doreen, an air hostess with Air Jamaica, were considered important enough to listen to whenever they spoke.

Aunty Chunni and Aunty Dada were two Indian women who were not related to Josephine but whom she called Aunty. They lived across the street and were sisters and good friends with Josephine's mother. They very often gave an eye on the children and watched over Josephine and Carla, ensuring that the children were safe at night. Their opinion was significant to Josephine's mother, too. They all thought Josephine's mother should not allow a little girl to do what Josephine was doing. They thought that it was useless to care for a crippled animal. They also thought feeding and cleaning such a creature was unsanitary.

Concerned adults kept repeating this advice to Josephine's mother to get her to persuade Josephine to stop looking after her pet. Thankfully, Josephine's mother did not insist that her daughter stop caring for the puppy. She listened and nodded in agreement; sometimes, Josephine's mother would admonish Josephine in their presence to appease the complaining adults. However, Josephine and her mother shared a bond regarding loving animals and those less fortunate. Josephine knew that her mother lacked the conviction to follow through on her threats to spank her or to get rid of her puppy.

Things even got worse as Josephine developed sores on her chin; now, with an adult understanding of bacteria, she understands why. Josephine's mother still did not interfere. Indeed, Josephine's chin was the site of an unsightly mass of sores. These sores elicited much scorn from school friends and renewed reprimands from the complaining adults who knew of Josephine's activities with her puppy. Teachers and Sunday School workers also expressed genuine care and concern for Josephine's well-being and wondered if Josephine needed to go to the doctor. Josephine cannot remember if Mama or Papa took her to the doctor. Still, she does recall being embarrassed because her mother painted her chin with *Gentian Violet,* a purple-coloured antiseptic, antibacterial dye that she felt made her look foolish at school with purple paint on her chin.

In childlike innocence, Josephine persevered and kept on with her labour of love.

Puppy kept licking Josephine's face, especially her chin, so as not to be outdone. Once again, childhood memory meets adult understanding in that a dog's ability to lick its wound promotes the healing of the wound. It seems Josephine had become kindred with the puppy, or so the puppy thought. Eventually, Josephine's chin healed completely. Nevertheless, it seemed as if the whole cycle of praying, feeding, cleaning and playing with the puppy lasted a long time.

During the rainy season, Josephine had to be especially vigilant to get home quickly because, inevitably, her puppy would be left in a puddle after the rain fell while she was at school. Then, without thought, she would take him in her arms, dry him with her uniform, clean and feed him and then pray that he would walk.

On what seemed like an ordinary evening, under a bright blue sky and in the sticky heat, Josephine ran home in the 3 pm Jamaican sun. Walking home from school was usually a hot and thirsty endeavour, especially for Josephine, who was too young to make significant steps, making Payne Avenue seem long. As usual, as she reached her gate, she looked down toward where her puppy was lying. He, too, had been looking out for her and from about a hundred yards away, Josephine realised that the most wondrous thing was happening.

Josephine's puppy saw her coming, and as if in slow motion, he began to rise onto his legs. Slowly and with much physical effort, he could stand, first with his two front legs and then, shaking and staggering, the hind legs were made straight. The puppy was standing!

The look on her puppy's face said, "Look at me, this is for you!" Josephine was dumbstruck! She ran to him in awe and wonder at what she was witnessing. She was so happy; her puppy seemed even more happy. He was by then staggering around on legs that were unnaturally long and thin for his body. It had happened! Jesus had answered Josephine's prayers! The wonder of the moment was profound. There was a God! He does answer prayers, and He loves puppies. Jesus can fix things. Life was so busy for all the adults that this became a passing incident to them. They acknowledged that the puppy had recovered but soon forgot about it. He was just another dog running around in the yard.

As Josephine grew up, so too did her faith in God. Neither Josephine nor the puppy on that day knew that together, they had just participated in a miracle.

However, Josephine's faith in God had taken on new wings. She could never look at those less fortunate than herself in the same way. Now, she could pray for people, and she did. Sometimes, she would pray after stopping to check in with someone or just sensing that they needed Jesus. Josephine especially loved and still does ask Jesus to send His angels to minister to neglected animals and little children on the street. Understanding that God is always willing, she asks Him for help.

Josephine remembers that Angels ministered to Jesus while He was tested in the desert. God will certainly do that for innocent animals and children.

Looking back, Josephine has grown up and fondly remembers her little puppy. Josephine's memory of this puppy after their mutual miracle has faded somewhat, but she does recall moving house for the third time from Payne Avenue to Spanish Town Road. Soon after the move, her Mama came home from work and found the puppy lying beside a sleeping Josephine.

The puppy, now a grown dog, had been left with the neighbours at Payne Avenue, and on his own, he found his way to Josephine's new home. Josephine's family now lived in an upstairs apartment, which they shared with a dental office and a tailor shop. The puppy had travelled about a mile and a half into the new yard and up the stairs to where Josephine was sleeping.

Josephine loved the puppy, and he loved her. She came to realise that animals do experience feelings. She knows that they smile when they are happy and their eyes reflect sadness when they are sad. Animals love without boundaries. This experience of caring for her puppy has been one of the most valuable of Josephine's life lessons.

Have you ever wondered if Jesus was real or if He would listen to your prayers? Josephine's story is true; she prayed to Him, and He listened to her when no one else would.

Her crippled puppy walked, and this created a childhood memory so intense that Josephine has never forgotten it.

Glossary

Anchor Butter - An imported brand of butter that was considered the best butter on the market.

Bully Beef - A popular brand of canned corned beef.

Cheese Krunches - a popular brand of locally baked savoury cheese flavoured, square shaped biscuits.

Excelsior Crackers - A popular brand of locally baked water crackers.

Gentian Violet - Gentian violet is an antiseptic dye used to treat fungal infections of the skin (such as ringworm, athlete's foot). It also has weak antibacterial effects.

Susumba - A bitter-tasting green peasized berry, also known as Gully Bean, Turkey Berry, Plate Brush, Devil Fig, Pea Eggplant, and many others.

THE YELLOW HAT

Josephine had a favourite couple that lived in the *tenement yaad,* where she lived with her family. This couple had the most favourable impression on her. They were married when most other couples were not. They were so different from everyone else in the *yaad* that they seemed out of place. They had lived in England before and had returned with different manners. Jamaicans were quick to say, "*Howdy, tenky* and *how yu du*?" This means hello, thanks, and how are you? They spoke in loud, hurried and confident voices, but this couple spoke in softer tones and said, "Thank you, hello, and how are you?" They spoke more slowly and waited for the answers before they spoke again. Even when they did join in corporate chatter under the mango tree, they spoke English rather than Jamaican Patwah. They seemed secure, happy and content. They attended church regularly, and the other tenants seemed to respect them more than they respected other people.

Mr. Francis had a steady job as a janitor at the Kingston Public Hospital and rode a bicycle. He was short, not very dark in complexion, and Josephine recalls Mama saying, "Mr Francis _hav_ fine features _an gud_ hair." Josephine thought that fine features and good hair meant that he was good-looking and his hair was not very thick. She supposed that her mother was right. Mr Francis always wore a hat, and his shirt was tucked into his pants, which were usually hemmed into a cuff. He seemed to be wearing his '_gud clothes_' all the time.

His wife was a homemaker who cared for her family by cooking, cleaning and meeting their needs. She was darker and fatter than he was. She had thick, woollen hair braided with untidy plaits that looked ugly to Josephine. Josephine recalls having the urge to fix the plaits and have them all go in the same direction. Mrs Francis had regular features; *she* was not beautiful but not ugly either. She wore an apron, which impressed Josephine very much as she had only seen that on television. Mrs Francis also knew how to cook well; Josephine recalls enjoying the food when invited for dinner. The Francis family had clean rooms, and took good care of their daughter. This kind of adult attentiveness impressed Josephine as she and Carla started cleaning their rooms when they were very young, as their mother was usually at work. Occasionally, Mrs Francis would buy extra fruit at the market and set up a stall from which she sold the fruits. This enterprise eventually grew into a shop selling bread and other necessities when they bought the yard.

Josephine liked this family and enjoyed spending time with them. At times, when they had her over for dinner, they sat together and ate after giving God thanks. Josephine would visit the Francis's for many years, even after she moved away, and they always welcomed her.

They also had the respect of the landlord as, unlike some of the other tenants, they could consistently produce the rent when he came to collect it. The landlord's respect for them was so evident that one day when he came to collect the rent, the Francises could not pay him. He listened sympathetically and expressed that he was sorry for the situation that they described. They told him that their daughter Janet had cut herself badly a few days before while playing. She had tried to retrieve a ball by pushing her arm through a barbed wire fence. She had sustained a serious cut to her forearm. They had used the rent to take her to the private doctor's office on Waltham Park Road for stitches. Josephine recalls well the day when Mrs Francis saw her daughter's arm. She looked alarmed, quickly put a hat on the child's head, and left, presumably taking her to the doctor.

Josephine always admired the way that Mrs Francis dressed up her daughter Janet. She wished she, too, could have a 'going out' hat to wear on Sundays when Mrs Francis invited her to go with them to church. Josephine waited impatiently all evening until her Mama came home from work to plead with her to buy her a hat for church.

Screech... clang! Upon hearing the sound of the gate, Josephine bolted towards the front gate to greet Mama. Tired as Mama was, she listened to Josephine's animated request. She sat in the doorway, looked deeply into her daughter's pleading eyes and thought about where the money would come from. Josephine beat her to it. "I found a shilling once while walking home, and I saved it. Look!" Tin -Tin's heart warmed toward her little girl, and was proud of her thriftiness. "Alright, I will make up the rest and ask Mrs Francis to take you shopping. *She know betta 'bout them sort of things. Awright, ma'am?*" Mama reassuringly promised her. Josephine was so happy she couldn't sleep until it was hat shopping day with Mrs Francis.

Josephine came into the hat shop, small, shy and intent only on getting a hat for Sunday school. Her mom had asked Mrs Francis to take her shopping for a church hat. Despite being overwhelmed by the sights and sounds of travelling on the JOS bus to downtown Kingston, Josephine felt excited; not even the prospect of getting "carsick' could dampen her excitement. You see, the smell of the fuel on the bus and the crowds of the downtown area would sometimes overstimulate Josephine, and she would vomit. This carsickness was always a disquiet for her and her mom. Mama had tried stuffing newspaper into Josephine's bosom before, as this was supposed to help stop the nausea and vomiting. It did not help and made

Josephine feel silly anyway. Today, the only remedy was the hope and the excitement of getting a new hat.

Mrs. Francis was an excellent example of a Christian to the other tenants in Josephine's yard. She was married when most other women were not. She and her husband had raised their daughter to believe in Jesus. They attended church regularly and had a stable home life. Mrs Francis sometimes took the children of other neighbours to church. They were informally the family that other families emulated. Josephine liked the Francis family and enjoyed learning from them. Her introduction to different Christian denominations came through her association with them. She attended the *St Peter Claver Roman Catholic Church,* on Waltham Park Road with them and the *Wildman Street Pentecostal Church* later.

Josephine grew up in an era when adults were very authoritarian. They believed that 'children should be seen but not heard.' This idiom meant children were told what to do and when and where to be. Josephine found that this went against her instincts. She was obedient but had questions that she mainly asked herself as she found that the adults dismissed her. "*gwaan go sit down, yu* ask *tu* much question." Or those like her parents who did not think about the questions too seriously would say, '*Mi nu* know, we'll see.' Josephine often felt like she was not being taken seriously by the adults in her life.

So even though *Tin-Tin* agreed that Josephine needed a hat, Josephine dreaded the process as she wanted to have a part in choosing her hat. She hoped that Mrs Francis would allow her to help choose it. All these emotions were going through her mind as she sat on the bus beside Mrs Francis. "Don't bite your nails, Josephine," said Mrs Francis. Josephine put her hands under her legs to stop herself from biting her nails. As they walked to the store, she was still nervous. "Why are you so quiet, Josephine?" Mrs Francis asked kindly. Josephine looked up at Mrs Francis and smiled sheepishly. "Nothing, Mrs Francis," she said. Eventually, they got to the store, and a new set of sensations assailed Josephine's consciousness. She felt like she had stepped inside a 'hat world'.

Momentarily, Josephine felt submerged in this new world. There were so many hats! Josephine looked at all the hats on display: the sensible whites, pale blues and beige hats. There were small hats, big hats, more oversized hats with wide floppy brims, and whippy hats with mesh to cover the face! Josephine had never noticed before a store that sold only hats! Sensing that Josephine was in shock, Mrs. Francis asked, 'Are you okay, Josephine?'

"Yes, Ma'am," She said.

"What about this white hat? It's appropriate," showing Josephine a hat that her daughter Janet usually wore. Josephine smiled hesitantly at Mrs Francis, recovering a bit from being overwhelmed. Josephine's independent way of thinking said with her 'inside voice,' *No, dem going to tink me falla fashing after Janet.*

Instead of blurting out how she actually felt, looking wide-eyed into Mrs Francis's kind face, she asked, "What does appropriate mean?"

"It means suitable," said Mrs Francis.

Patiently, Mrs. Francis picked up a pale blue hat and admired and touched the lace and ribbons. She told her little charge, "Feel this, Josephine, look at how pretty this hat is." Josephine obediently felt the texture of the hat, feigning interest. She looked around again, still searching with her eyes and testing with her hands among the array of hats.

Josephine agreed, "*Yes, it's nice,*" but she found her little heart was not agreeing with her lips as her eyes kept on searching. She was getting more comfortable now as Mrs Francis was not forcing her to take just any hat. Josephine was so used to adults doing that. She felt the tension leaving her body as she felt free to peruse the displays. Suddenly, her heart said; *Here is your hat!* Josephine became lost in the reverie of what she saw.

Josephine's sight had landed on a yellow hat! You see, Josephine loved the colour yellow. Mama talked of loving the colour yellow, too. The colour was vibrant and reminiscent of an empty Topaz perfume bottle with an amber-coloured gem on top that Josephine had seen by her grandmother's house. Josephine loved the way the gem on the bottle would pick up the light and give off a warm, amber hue on *Granny Mum's* dresser. She wasn't concerned about the sense of the occasion for the hat, that being church. At only seven years old, Josephine was not bothered by reasoning or fashion trends. She fell in love with the yellow hat on the spot. She did not know about coordinating colours. It did not occur to her that her yellow hat would not match her red church dress. To her, the yellow hat was simply the best because it was yellow. Immediately, she was busy imagining herself wearing it with her red dress to church.

"Josephine... Josephine... Josephine, are you listening? Mrs Francis inquired of Josephine, who was so lost in her imagination that when she heard Mrs Francis' voice, it was as if it was coming from far away. Coming back from her reverie, Josephine quickly answered, "Yes, Mrs Francis."

"Is this the hat that you want?" Asked Mrs Francis, picking up the yellow hat.

"Yes, please," said Josephine, clapping her hands excitedly.

Mrs Francis placed the hat on Josephine's head and made her look at herself in the mirror. Josephine's heart sang along with the angels that Josephine was hearing in her head. Suddenly, the world was happy; Josephine's heart and eyes were happy, too.

After asking her if she was sure, Mrs Francis paid for the hat, and the saleswoman placed it inside a nice new paper bag and handed it to Josephine. Mrs Francis did not point out why it should not be the yellow hat. She had only suggested the paler colours. Josephine liked this about Mrs Francis and felt that, finally, an adult was taking her seriously and that she was *'big'* enough to make a decision.

The hat was sunflower yellow, bright and new. Made from faux straw, its 'new' smell was not usually experienced by Josephine, except at Christmas time when she would receive a plastic toy. New toys were usually bought at the Christmas Market in downtown Kingston, and the smell of 'new things' was irrepressible in Josephine's mind. Today's sensation was a mixture of the excitement of her purchase and the memory of Christmas Market shopping. It was like Christmas had come in July.

The hat's pale yellow ribbons danced and flirted with the gentle breezes, highlighting its bright yellow hue. Josephine imagined herself in a story, holding her yellow hat on a windy day. The hat's wide brim cast a shadow over Josephine's face while providing the benefit of the shade against the sun, fulfilling the purpose of its design. It seemed to Josephine that its brim was proud to encircle her face, as it appeared to be smiling broadly, causing her a permanent sense of well-being. The box-top of the hat, which had extra shiny silk-like padding inside, majestically stood as a sentry against the heat of the sun's rays, dutifully absorbing its warmth and reflecting its glow.

Oh, the simple wonders that make children thrive confidently! Josephine felt lighter than air when she wore her yellow hat. The Yellow hat coloured Josephine's world in beautiful tones of happiness; a light shone all around, and faces seemed kind and friendly as Josephine viewed her world from under the brim of her hat. Josephine's heart said *You look beautiful!' Everyone loves your hat. I can't wait to wear my hat again next week,* she told herself, touching her hat shyly as the Sunday School teacher spoke about Noah and the Flood, then Jonah in the Whale.

So, week after week, Sunday after Sunday, Josephine wore her yellow hat to Sunday School. In Josephine's heart, her yellow hat was perfect with every dress. She felt special, proud and confident when she wore her hat. Going to Sunday School became a thrill due to this simple fact: **Josephine loved wearing her yellow hat.**

Today, the memory of that yellow hat is still vivid. Its ribbons are still dancing, its brim is shading, and its box top is still protecting. Together, they chorus: Simple childlikeness can teach life's more complex lessons of purpose, happy contentment, eager willingness and pleased confidence. After all, a hat is still a hat despite its colour, and Josephine was delighted that hers was yellow.

Dedicated to my daughter Rachel Erin, who triggered the memory and inspired the story. Her innocent and wonderful childlike perspective often caused me to pause and see things differently.

Glossary

Good Clothes/gud clothes - Clothes worn only for going out, formal, nicer clothes, not worn around the house to lounge or play in.

Howdy - How do you do?

Tenky - Thank you!

How Yu Du? - How are you doing?

JOS - The Jamaica OmniBus Service operated a municipal bus service for the Kingston Metropolitan area from 1953 to 1983.

Wikipedia.https://en.m.wikipedia.org

MISS SHEILA
IN RELIEF

A regular 12 o'clock whistle was sounded at the **Salada Foods Coffee Factory**. Situated south of the tenement *yaad* at Bell Road off the Spanish Town Road, it was founded in 1958 and is one of Jamaica's largest **Blue Mountain Coffee** processing plants. The sound of the whistle signalled that all was well. The coffee was processed and dried, resulting in a familiar aroma. To this day, the smell of a cup of coffee transports Josephine right back to those beautiful days under the mango tree in the tenement *yaad* when she would hear the coffee factory whistle blow and inhale the wafts of roasted coffee beans that filled the air.

It was usually not long after the afternoon sun cooled off a bit that some salespeople regularly came into Josephine's *yaad* to transact business: People such as the peanut lady, Mr Barker, who sold meat, the salesman who sold books and Encyclopaedias, the life Insurance salesman, and Miss Sheila, who sold clothes and household articles out of her bags. These regulars enjoyed a convivial relationship with the residents in the tenement *yaad*, developing mutual trust.

The peanut lady, for instance, once asked to take all the children to church with her, and the parents agreed. Josephine recalls wondering about her church as it was held under a big tree around which the peanut lady had to march several times with the children marching behind her. She and the other church members made heavy chanting sounds, carried flags in red, green, and black, and wore white clothes with their heads wrapped up in cloth and into which pencils were stuck. Josephine did not think this was a 'safe' outing and didn't treat the peanut lady after that with much regard.

Miss Sheila, however, had the most lasting impression on Josephine among all the passing salespeople who visited the tenement *yaad*. She came to conduct business with the women of the *yaad* once every two weeks, usually on a Wednesday. It is funny how Josephine seemed to have had, as a child, a built-in timing device without knowing how to tell the time or even being interested in the time of day. She usually expected to see Miss Sheila when she appeared.

Miss Sheila's wig was never on her head quite straight, usually askew with kinky hair sticking out at the back and sides as if her natural hair was attempting to escape.

Miss Sheila and her Caucasian-looking wig could be seen coming from West Anderson Crescent, having walked from Waltham Park Road via Howard Avenue or Espeut Avenue in the midday sun.

She was different from the other women, not just in how she appeared but also in how she presented herself. As she sweated down the road towards Josephine's yard on Payne Avenue, her face was garishly painted 60s style with shades of cosmetics that were too pale for a black woman. Mopping her face delicately so as not to smudge her foundation colour, she carried a heavy bag where she sold the wares. Miss Sheila's style was inspired by places beyond the shores of Jamaica. She wore her strange hair and face confidently, plus accessories like scarves, plastic beads and earrings. Her Jewellery was too shiny to be real, and her clothes were meant for cooler temperatures.

There were no living rooms within which to entertain Miss Sheila. Instead, all the women would gather around her beneath the shady mango tree, and there, they would transact business, bringing a hive of activity to the tenement *yaad*. Sometimes, Miss Sheila would ask for a glass of water and other times, someone would offer her a drink of lemonade. She would fan herself while unpacking her bag to showcase her goods. Her bag had a fantastic capacity to hold many things:- Underwear, blouses, shirts, skirts, pants, scented bath soaps, fancy furry bedroom shoes for children with animal heads, plastic scrub- brushes, sheets, towels, and even pots and pans.

Miss Sheila also had a book in which she recorded the amounts owed to her and hoped to collect from the women. On those days, all the women enjoyed looking at the new things that came out of Miss Sheila's bag; many asked the prices of particular items, but not many could afford to purchase them. Certainly, Josephine recollects that Miss Sheila usually gave items on credit until the next fortnight.

Miss Sheila was a good salesperson; she adeptly pointed out the better quality of the fabrics on the clothes she was selling. She knew who she could prevail upon to 'trust' the goods until she returned to collect, and she encouraged them by reminding them that if they had bought the items singly in the store, they would pay more. Mis Sheila shopped wholesale and was giving wholesale prices. Her clothes lasted long and did not lose colour, fade or tear; she never missed an opportunity to use herself as an example.

Miss Sheila was a keen businesswoman collecting outstanding balances and recording new amounts owed. If someone was unable to pay the expected amount or if they asked for a discount, Miss Sheila had several responses, all surrounding the fact that she did not have a man. So, it was not unusual to hear her say, *"You better than me you know, you have a man, I don't,"* or *"I don't have a man to help me, you know."*

Being around her mother and the other women, Josephine heard them mimic Miss Sheila outside of her presence. *"Kekekekke, Woie, Miss Sheila want a man."* They would laugh and say. Of course, what was so sad was her assumption that the women there were better off than her, and the reason for that assumption was, in most cases, entirely incorrect. Most of the women were struggling to feed their children despite having male partners.

Miss Sheila was independent, enterprising and free to be whomever she wanted. Well ahead of her time, she was one of Josephine's first observations of an emerging class of women and men who came to be known in Jamaica in the 1970s as **Informal Commercial Importers or Higglers.** They carved out a place within the middle class for themselves and their families as they travelled abroad to shop and returned home to sell their goods. This became their means to pull themselves up in society. They could purchase homes, send their children to better schools and even set themselves up in other businesses.

Josephine did not know Miss Sheila's last name or where she lived; she just came once every two weeks. She was not a friend to any of the women in the yaad, just a business associate who would come and go. Among the women who bought her wares was a young woman named Thelma, who lived with a man named Slim Lloydy. She was cocky and worldly. Quick to get into a quarrel and even a fight. Thelma was short, muscular and fair-skinned and wore her street smarts manners like a badge of honour. *"A outta east mi come from,"* She boasted, suggesting that hailing from the East made her tougher than others. Josephine later learned Thelma was only 17 years old and that 'East' was Windward Road and its environs.

Thelma told fanciful tales to Carla and *Juwan* who hung on to her every word and later related them to Josephine. She entertained them with stories of proper gentlemen suitors who opened doors, pulled out chairs for her, and treated her like a princess. Her stories were inconsistent with the actual situation that Thelma lived in and more in keeping with what Josephine had heard about in fairy tales. *A*

pure lie Thelma a tell, don't it, Mango Tree?
Said Josephine to the mango tree in suspicion.

Thelma would '*trust*' Miss Sheila's goods and often could not afford to pay her. Since '*trusting*' meant taking goods on credit and paying later, this was always a stern test of integrity.

One day, while Miss Sheila was walking down the road towards the tenement *yaad,* Thelma, seeing her, went and hid in her room. When Miss Sheila had finished setting up her wares, she pulled out her book to start collecting her debts.

"Tanks, Ms Francis. I can always count on you," she said as she wrote down the amount Mrs Francis had paid her.

"*You sure dis is all you have fi mi?*" She asked Josephine's mother, Tin-Tin, turning the pages in her book to her name. Having verified the amount, she said, "*Oh, alright.*"

"*Tanks, Beryl, you should take that red skirt. Is your size, and is it a wear, nowadays.*" She encouraged Miss Beryl.

"*Mi ago, try it on and come back,*" said Miss Beryl, walking away with her skirt tucked under her arm.

As the transactions went on, Miss Sheila collected and then encouraged someone to '*trust*' this item or that. It suddenly occurred to Miss Sheila that Thelma was missing. "*Wey Thelma deh? A de second time me a come yah and she no dey yah, she owe mi nuff money and every time mi come, mi caan collect,*" said Miss Sheila.

Miss Beryl was just returning from trying on the red skirt, when she heard Miss Sheila's enquiry. "*Yes, wey Thelma disappear to? She was right here so earlier,*" said Miss Beryl. The other women did not answer but pretended they had not heard the questions.

Then Mrs. Francis said calmly, "She went into her room." This energised Miss Beryl: *"Wa? No man, she need to come talk to Miss Sheila,'* she insisted. After which Miss Beryl proceeded to knock on Thelma's door. *"Thelma, come talk to Miss Sheila, mi done tell you sey you mustn't trust the woman tings if you caan afford dem. You too red-eye and covetous! Come out here right now and talk to Miss Sheila."* She demanded while pounding heavily on Thelma's door.

Miss Beryl was the voice of authority in the tenement *yaad* and a 'KNOWN beater,' so the other women held their breaths as they knew that Thelma was brash and rude and thought she was tough too. For her part, Miss Sheila was busy reminding the other women that she did not have a man to help her and was alone. *"Uno know seh, is me one,* trying to make ends meet.*"* After several minutes of Miss Beryl knocking on the door and berating Thelma, the door flew open, and Thelma stepped out unapologetically. With her petite frame erect and chest puffed out, Thelma looked ready to start trading insults with Miss Beryl. However, before a proper *tracing match* or fight could start, Thelma suddenly seemed to realise that she was outmatched in every way by Miss Beryl, 'The Beater.'

"*Wey you a bring down scandal pon mi fa? Mi a no tief yu know,*" said Thelma, placating Miss Beryl. "*Nobadi nu sey yu a tief but come talk to Sheila. She want ar money,*" said Miss Beryl, unmoved.

"*Yu a no mi mada; you caan talk to mi soh; mi a no yu pickney,*" said Thelma.

Quickly turning away from Beryl towards Miss Sheila, she asked in an affected voice, "*How much mi owe you, Sheila?*" "Seven dollars," said Miss Sheila.

Thelma dug her fingers into her bra and pulled out three bills: two $2.00 notes and a $1.00 note.

"*Tek dis. Mi wi give yu di balance next time,*" she said, storming off. "*Mi a nu tief and mi nay run wey,*" She *threw the words behind her,* flouncing off.

Mrs Francis followed her to calm her down and encouraged her not to 'trust goods' as she would have to make the payments at some time. The other women were also consoling Miss Beryl, who was visibly upset. "*Mi nuh know a whe Slim Lloydy tek up wid dis ya likkle caa'less, renking tail gal, fa.*" If a neva fi 'im yu see...ahhhh bway! Unu know whe she woulda get.*"

"*Alright Beryl, yu sey yu piece and yu get the result, neva mind now,*" Said Josephine's mother, Tin-Tin.

"*No man, she fi do better dan dat.*" Said Miss Beryl, "*Sheila a tun ar hand at sumting, yu have fi encourage ar. You caan carry dung the oman business.*"

Miss Shelia broke the tension. *"Beryl, mi can always depend pon yu."*

"Miss Tin Tin, Mrs Francis, tanks to unu, mi get some ting an it betta dan nothing."

"Miss Beryl, di skirt fit you?"

As the tension died down, the women resumed their light banter and interaction with Miss Sheila. Mrs Francis had the proper state of commerce in the yard rectified, and Miss Sheila continued to bring her goods to sell to the women for a long time. Josephine's impression was that women are strong, inventive, and resilient. Miss Sheila was hard-working, spunky and enterprising. The other women had integrity, backbone and grit. They found amusement even in their dire circumstances. The women knew when to *'give laugh for peas soup'* and when something was no laughing matter... Big excitement in the yaad is one thing, but a big war is something else. That nobody wanted!

Miss Beryl and Thelma both had the moxie to challenge someone else. Beryl was mature enough to know how far to take a quarrel. Thelma, however, was still young and immature. Sadly, she paid the ultimate price by rushing into a fight with someone else and losing her life early.

Mrs Francis and Tin-Tin had the spirit of compassion and were the usual peacemakers who calmed the others' ruffled feathers when needed. These women impressed Josephine so much that they created a lasting memory. Miss Sheila was a trailblazer, and Josephine hoped that she would go on to be numbered among those who could cross social barriers and carve out better lives for themselves.

This is dedicated to the superhero women of my youth: TinTin, Beryl, Mrs. Francis, and Ms. Sheila. Their indomitable spirits still live on in Jamaican women all over the world.

Glossary

Blue Mountain Coffee - A world class variety of Arabica coffee bean that is grown in the high altitudes of the Jamaican Blue Mountain.

Moxie - strength of character, determination, courage

Trus - when a salesperson trusts you to take goods on credit or defer payment for a specific agreed time.

'To Give laugh for peas soup' - To joke around and have a good time

To Throw word behind you - Jamaican meaning to walk away having addressed someone without acknowledging them directly

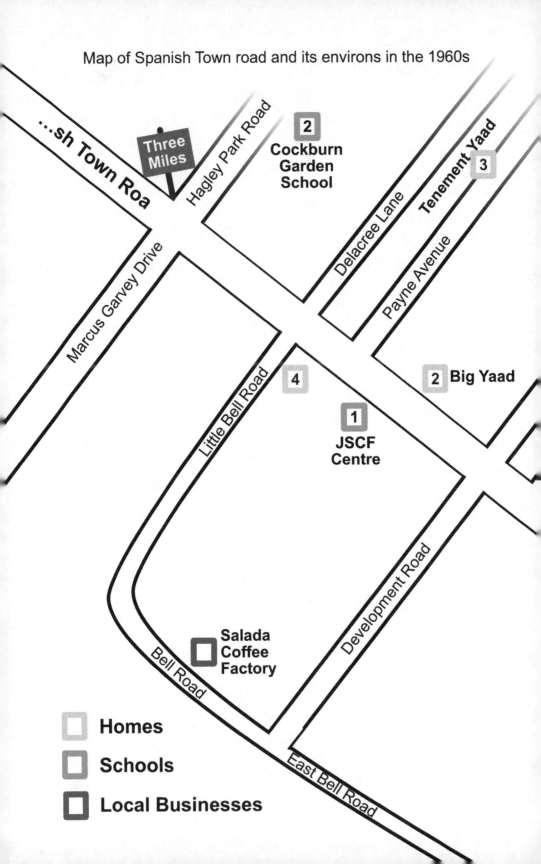

Map of Spanish Town road and its environs in the 1960s

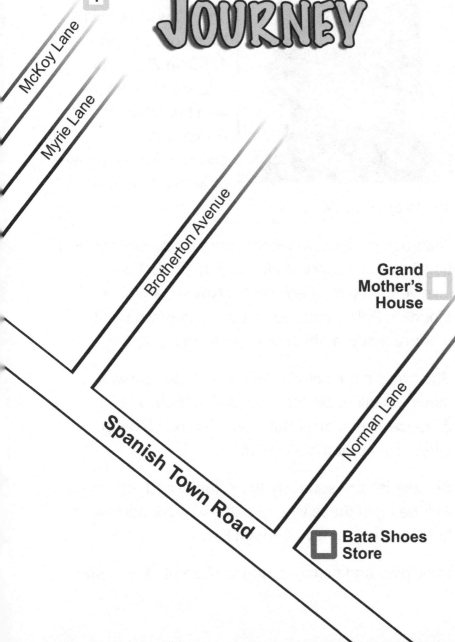

About The Author

Joan Pamela McDonald Hamilton (affectionately known to her friends as "Joey") was born in Kingston, Jamaica 1960. In 2000, she migrated to Canada with her husband, Arthur and three children. Her odyssey of writing began after she left her homeland.

Joan has enjoyed vocational pursuits as diverse as banking, missionary work and Sunday School involvement over many years, Royal Canadian Mounted Police contractor, businesswoman and, more recently, author over a few decades.

She holds a bachelor's degree in Theology with a minor in Guidance and Counselling from The Jamaica Theological Seminary and has a deep interest in human behaviour.

She takes very seriously the spiritual and emotional well-being of those whose paths interconnect with hers as she journeys through life.

Principled and caring for the welfare of others, she

endeavours to help others in need and young persons achieve their everyday, short-term, or career objectives through personal mentoring.

Joan became a Christian at the age of 15 years and found that her relationship with Christ is the foundation upon which her feet are most sure. She currently resides in St Andrew, Jamaica, where she continues to enjoy writing.

Made in the USA
Monee, IL
20 March 2024

55445218R00125